complete
paint &
wall coverings

Consulting Editor: Don Vandervort

Staff for this Book:

Editor: Rob Lutes

Art Director: Odette Sévigny

Assistant Editors: Stacey Berman, Ned Meredith

Researcher: Adam van Sertima

Designer: Hélène Dion

Picture Editor: Linda Castle

Production Editor: Brian Parsons

Production Coordinator: Dominique Gagné

Systems Director: Edward Renaud

Scanner Operators: Martin Francoeur, Sara Grynspan

Technical Support: Jean Sirois

Indexer: Linda Cardella Cournoyer

Book Consultants:

Margi Barnes

Skip Lennox

Complete Paint & Wall Coverings was produced in conjunction with

ST. REMY MULTIMEDIA

Cover:

Photographer: Phil Harvey

Photo Director: JoAnn Masaoka Van Atta

Original design by Urban Design Group of Denver, CO

Adapted by Pacific Peninsula Architecture of Menlo Park, CA

Interior Design: Coliene Brennan, Brenco Designs of Menlo Park, CA

Cover Designer: Vasken Guiragossian

VP, Editorial Director, Sunset Books: Bob Doyle

For additional copies of *Complete Paint & Wall Coverings*, or any
other Sunset book, call 1-800-526-5111, or visit our website
at www.sunset books.com.

complete
paint &
wall coverings

Sunset

Table of Contents

The World of COLOR AND DESIGN

Whether you hang colorful wallpaper in a bathroom or put a fresh coat of paint on your home's exterior, redecorating your walls with paint and wall coverings will have a dramatic effect on any space. Whatever combination of colors, patterns, and textures you end up with will determine to a large extent the overall character of your home. With this in mind, it's crucial that you examine your options carefully and make choices that you will be able to live with—and enjoy—for years to come. Remember, good design doesn't happen by accident. It is the result of a careful process of selecting and arranging materials in a way that is both functional and aesthetically pleasing. The following chapter will help you come up with a decorating scheme that meets these criteria. Sections on decorating your walls, creating with color, and the rules of design will help demystify the decorating process and help you achieve the look you want. Finally, information on working with professionals will give you tips on hiring someone to come up with a plan or to do the work for you.

This wall covering's diamond motif is echoed in the room's curtains, lending a sense of order to a cozy dining space.

Decorating Your Walls

When decorating with paint and wall coverings, think of your home's indoor and outdoor surfaces as canvases to be covered in a way that suits your style, fashion sense, and color preferences. The decisions you make, while not irreversible, are important. They will affect how you feel about your home.

Whether adding a subtle decorative touch or completely redesigning your surroundings, the choices at your disposal are vast. As you begin the planning process, look to homes and buildings around you for ideas. Home-improvement centers, decorators' show houses, paint and wallpaper stores, and fabric stores also often feature displays highlighting styles of paint and wall coverings.

INTERIOR/EXTERIOR DECORATING

How you approach the task of decorating depends largely on whether you are working on your home's interior or exterior.

Decorating interiors: When selecting an indoor color scheme, consider first the natural lighting in the room—generally, darker rooms benefit from light-colored walls. Light- or cool-colored walls also tend to expand a room visually. Furnishings also play an important role. For good design, walls and furniture must work hand in hand.

Match the wall covering to the room's use as well as to its appearance. Every product has practical as well as aesthetic qualities. Delicate fabric may not be highly suited to a child's room, for example, where fingerprints, spills, and

other mishaps are inevitable, so choose a wall covering that will accommodate your child's lifestyle. In every room, take into account the condition of the bare walls. Some coverings are more suitable for less than perfectly smooth walls, whereas others demand a completely smooth surface.

Specific rooms also have special decorative requirements. Infant's rooms, for example, should be done in bright primary and secondary colors. When decorating youngsters' rooms with paint and wall coverings, don't neglect the ceiling—it's a great place to feature vibrant colors and designs.

Decorating exteriors: When repainting the exterior of your home, bear in mind that the design of the home and its setting are dominant features. The colors you choose for the home must complement them. There are a few general rules that will help set you on the right path. First, don't opt for overly striking color combinations. You will have to look at the colors you choose for several years, so err on the conservative side and keep the colors simple and understated. Avoid what's known as the "dollhouse effect"—using colors that look too shiny and unreal. The colors of a home's siding, trim, doors, and even the roof should all complement each other to achieve a pleasant, relaxing appearance.

Often the architectural style of your home will dictate the colors you should choose. Small Queen Anne–style homes, for example, usually look best when painted light, neutral colors; larger homes

Whether the setting is highly decorative *(above)* or muted *(inset)*, good design is always immediately apparent.

Deep red, fabric-covered walls bring rich color and texture to this living room and provide a striking backdrop for furniture and accessories.

With its bright floral pattern, the wall covering in this bedroom creates a traditional, romantic look that's echoed in its ornate mirror and bureau.

can be painted slightly darker. Trim is traditionally a darker shade than that of the walls.

WALL COVERING OPTIONS

How you decorate also is largely influenced by the type of wall covering you decide to use.

Paint: The easiest and most economical way to transform a home's interior or exterior walls is by painting. Basic painting provides a uniform overall finish. Decorative techniques such as colorwashing, ragging, and sponging lend new vitality and depth to painted walls.

Wallpaper: Wallpapering has long been one of the most lasting and effective ways of reworking the style of a room. The variety of materials, styles, colors, patterns, and textures available is bedazzling—and opens up an entire world of decorating possibilities.

Wallpaper can add flair to sparsely decorated rooms or set a unifying style in busier spaces. By adding borders, you can add a hint of color to plain walls or complement an existing wall covering or paint job.

Fabric: For texture, warmth, beauty, color, and pattern, fabric provides another excellent choice. It has the added advantage of concealing minor wall imperfections.

Upholstered walls—fabric over backing material—are soft and luxurious, and provide some insulating and soundproofing qualities. Stapling and pasting fabric are simpler procedures for those applying fabric for the first time.

This Oriental-style dining room showcases simple form and furnishings—but is marked by walls painted a striking deep red.

Creating with Color

Color is the springboard for all design ideas. Decorating schemes are built around color, so you'll need to become familiar with color's intricacies.

When creating color schemes, don't be too shy to experiment. Color is subjective and emotional, so offbeat combinations and strong colors may work well—just consider the tastes of everyone who will have to live with the results.

Also keep in mind that to create a timeless appearance, it's best to avoid overly trendy colors and decorating schemes.

The following are some terms of color theory you should know.

Hue: Every hue—a synonym for color—has a visual temperature. Red, orange, and yellow are warm, lively hues, often called advancing colors because they seem nearer than they actually are. Cool, calm, receding colors—violet, green, and blue—appear farther away.

Intensity: This is a color's purity, strength, and saturation. For example, while both robin's egg and indigo are colors in the "blue family," they differ in their intensity. Increase intensity by adding pure color; reduce it with white, black, or the color's complement. Use strong, full-intensity colors mostly for decorative emphasis.

Value: This is the amount of light or dark in color. The more white present, the lighter is the value.

Tints, shades, and tones: The process of making tints, shades, or tones is called extending colors. Add white to a color to produce a tint. Tints lie just inside the color wheel's ring of hues (*opposite*). To make a shade (and darken the value), add black. Shades are found on the outer ring of the color wheel. Add gray to produce a color tone.

THE COLOR WHEEL

Although the colors in the wheel often appear intense, remember that you can soften their impact by combining and altering them.

All color combinations and variations can be found on the color wheel; use the wheel to help you picture colors together or to build various decorating schemes based on a few color preferences.

Primary colors: These are red, blue, and yellow, the source of all other colors. They are usually too powerful to use full strength on such large areas as bedroom walls.

Varying shades of cool, violet hues make this combined living/dining room appear more open and spacious.

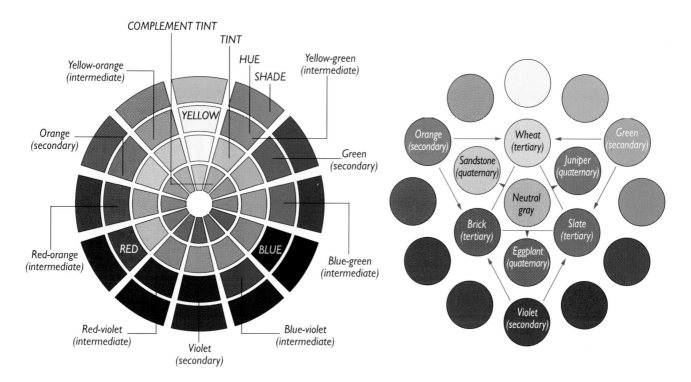

COMPLEMENT TINT
TINT
HUE
SHADE

Yellow-orange (intermediate)
Yellow-green (intermediate)
Orange (secondary)
Green (secondary)
YELLOW
Red-orange (intermediate)
RED
BLUE
Blue-green (intermediate)
Red-violet (intermediate)
Blue-violet (intermediate)
Violet (secondary)

Orange (secondary)
Wheat (tertiary)
Green (secondary)
Sandstone (quaternary)
Juniper (quaternary)
Neutral gray
Brick (tertiary)
Slate (tertiary)
Eggplant (quaternary)
Violet (secondary)

COLOR WHEEL AND CIRCLE

Use the color wheel *(above, left)* to help you picture how different colors will look together. If you have a definite color idea in mind, use of the wheel will expand your choices by allowing you to build up a number of different schemes.

The color circle *(above, right)* can help you see the different tertiary and quaternary colors that result from combining secondary or tertiary colors. For example, follow the arrows from secondary green and violet to see the result of mixing them—the tertiary slate. Combine tertiaries such as brick and slate to make eggplant, a quaternary.

Secondary colors: Formed from combinations of the stronger primary colors, these lie midway between primaries on the wheel: Green comes from blue and yellow, violet from red and blue, and orange from yellow and red.

Intermediate colors: These result from mixing a primary with an adjacent secondary color. For example, red and orange combine to make the intermediate red-orange.

Complementary colors: These lie opposite each other on the wheel, such as red and green. When mixed in equal amounts, they neutralize each other to form gray. But adding just a touch of its complement softens a color. These softened tints are on the color wheel's inner ring.

Tertiary and quaternary colors: These subtle versions of original colors have added depth and sophistication. And they're more interesting than shades.

Combining secondary colors produces a tertiary. Follow the arrows on the color circle above. For example, orange and green yield wheat. Note that varying amounts of white have been added to the tertiaries.

Combining tertiaries creates quaternaries. For example, wheat and brick yield sandstone; brick and slate create eggplant.

Neutral colors: These are white, black, and gray. Although not technically neutrals, low-intensity warm colors like beige and cream are usually included in neutral schemes. Light-value neutrals put the focus on the room, not the walls; they are ideal backgrounds for artwork.

ACCENTING WITH COLOR

Color highlights a room's structure and furnishings, and accentuates outdoor architectural features.

Indoors, ceiling beams, moldings, and chair rails gain prominence when stained or painted to contrast with walls and ceilings. Outdoors, contrasting window borders create bold effects.

Pick out a dominant color from a favorite element—a rug, couch, or flower box—then use that color, toned down, on indoor or outdoor walls. Lighter versions produce subtle effects; go darker for more drama. Use the next strong color on furniture or windows and the original item's accent in accessories. Be sure to vary the quantities of color and to repeat each one at least once.

Brighten accents with neutrals, but note that too sharp a contrast can be jarring. Inject vivid color only in small quantities, such as with a primary-colored sofa pillow.

COLOR SCHEMES

Room decor or pre-established outdoor style may already suggest a color scheme. Or, maybe you plan to combine favorite colors. In any case, understanding the three basic color schemes will help you devise your own. Remember that working colors likely will be softened versions of those on the wheel.

Monochromatic: These unified, restful schemes use one color in a variety of intensities and values. Accent colors and a mix of textures can keep the effect lively.

A neutral combination, a type of monochromatic scheme, consists of white, black, and very low intensities of colors like beige and taupe. Neutrals can be warm or cool; try to be consistent. Avoid monotony with a range of light-to-dark values.

COMPLEMENTARY COMBINATIONS

Involved complementary combinations produce more interesting color schemes. As shown at right, complementary hues opposite each other *(top left)* or triad colors equidistant on the color wheel *(top right)* can anchor a color scheme. You can further refine this triad to yield cocoa, sage, and dove gray. Further delve into color theory with a split complement *(bottom left)*; take one primary or intermediate color and add the colors on each side of its complement. For a double split complement, split both original colors in this same manner *(bottom right)*.

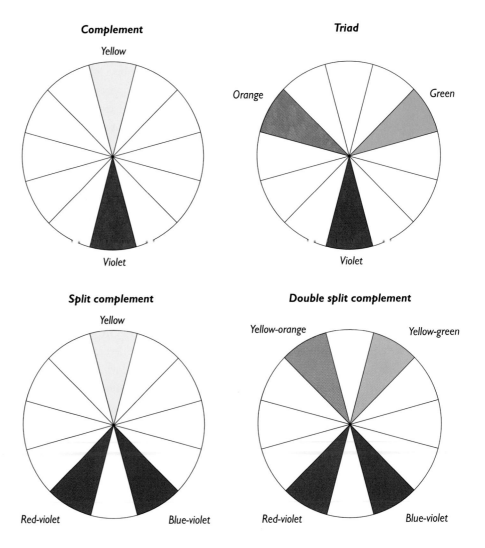

Old-English charm suffuses this warm yellow living room. Tile hearth accents complement the curtains and furniture while the sofa matches the wall color.

Complementary: These schemes are based on colors that are opposite to each other on the color wheel *(page 13)*. Their richness results from a balance of warm and cool colors. These mixes can be startling or subdued; consider a dining room with soft, amethyst window coverings and cream-colored walls.

Split complementaries for more complex combinations *(opposite)*: A triad consists of any three colors equidistant on the color wheel. A split complement has one primary or intermediate color plus the color on each side of its opposite. Split both sides of the wheel for a double split complement to produce four colors in a combination that's even more dynamic and harmonious. The resulting colors can further be refined and softened: In the example shown at bottom right on the opposite page, yellow-orange can become soft papaya, blue-violet

yields pale lavender blue, red-violet gives a quiet orchid, and yellow-green could become a light lime.

Vary complement intensity, value, and quantity to avoid the clash of pure opposing color. The most pleasing schemes usually result from neutralizing and extending colors in combination and using them in varied quantities. Most complementary combinations balance colors, ensuring harmony and preventing color chaos.

Analogous: Also called related schemes, these comprise two or more adjacent colors on the wheel.

The most agreeable analogous combinations contain colors that fall between two primaries and include one of those primaries—yellow-green, green, blue-green, and blue, for example. Just limit the number of colors to no more than four, with only one as the dominant color.

CHARACTERISTICS OF COLOR

Aside from trying to visualize how colors will work together—whether you're painting the interior or exterior of the house—there are some other factors affected by the colors you choose. Understanding these opens up a whole new world of design ideas.

Altering space with color: Visual temperature, value, and intensity all play a role in altering the sense of space in a room or area. Warm, advancing colors make a room appear smaller. Similarly, darker values (shades) of all colors diminish an area's size because they absorb light. More intense colors, whether warm or cool, also have this effect. You can use this knowledge to make a large space feel more cozy.

Make a housefront seem more dominating or open up a space with receding and low-intensity hues or unbroken expanses of light values.

Too much contrast has the same impact as a dark color—it reduces the perceived space. Enlarge space with harmonious analogous and monochromatic schemes. Neutrals of similar value also open up space, which emphasizes furnishings.

A ceiling the same color as the walls or lighter expands the space. A darker hue or one that continues for a distance down the walls visually lowers the ceiling for a more intimate atmosphere.

Light and color: The quality of light, natural or artificial, greatly affects color. Cool fluorescents weaken warm hues and amplify cool ones, whereas warm incandescent light yields the converse effect.

Reflected and tinted light raises the intensity of colors similar to that of the original object and neutralizes complementary colors.

Low light darkens value and reduces intensity. Too much light can make colors look washed out.

Color and mood: Color can energize or soothe. Red—the hottest of the warm colors—is usually too strong for relaxing rooms, such as the kitchen or bedroom. Sunshine colors like yellow and cream, as well as colors with light values and high intensities, raise spirits and brighten living spaces—they also mix easily with other colors. Use them in busy areas, such as dining rooms and children's rooms.

Use warm, dominant colors and those with light values to brighten up a dark room. In sunny rooms, use cooler colors and darker values to balance mood and cut glare.

Colors with medium values and intensities along with hues midway between warm and cool—yellow-green and red-violet, for example—have a relaxed, comforting effect. Cool, subdued colors, darker values, and low intensities are great for formal, restful rooms.

Consider a color's emotional impact when developing schemes. And remember that indoor and outdoor walls, by their size alone, make a strong statement, whatever their color or design.

Matching fabric wall covering and curtains unify the walls in this bedroom (left).

A blue wash applied in squares over a white base coat provides an eye-catching yet traditional backdrop to the rustic pantry at right.

Design Basics

An understanding of basic design elements and principles will help jump-start your decorating job. Although these concepts may seem abstract at first, keep them in mind as you develop your own style.

ELEMENTS OF DESIGN

Color may be first and foremost among the design elements, but also critical to a decorating scheme are space, line, texture, and pattern. These will help you achieve a balanced, beautiful effect.

Space: Walls enclose an indoor space and define an outdoor one. How space is perceived depends on color, line, texture, and pattern.

To increase the sense of space, leave some expanses of wall empty. Or, emphasize openings, such as pass-throughs and windows; these let the eye travel to other areas.

To make an area more intimate, subdivide an undefined space into distinct areas using contrasting color, texture, and pattern on walls, furnishings, or outdoor accents.

Line: The "lines" of a room refer to the room's shape or the dominant visual direction created by all the decorating elements. An area can include many lines, such as vertical, horizontal, diagonal, angular, and curved.

Vertical lines in striped wallpaper, for example, lend a sense of height and formality, whereas horizontal lines add informality. The isolated horizontal lines of a chair rail can break up wall expanses for a cozier atmosphere. Diagonal and

Yellow window, door, and porch trim and cornice moldings combine with the horizontal siding and angular roof lines to bring visual balance to this front facade.

The texture achieved with a blend of paint colors gives this functional wall of closets added aesthetic appeal.

angular lines suggest strong movement, while curves impart a gentler sense of motion and energy.

Texture: The smooth glow of paint and the softness of fabric are just two examples of texture on walls. Even wallpaper, whether textured or not, possesses visual texture.

Texture on walls is a subtle refiner of color. The smooth, shiny surface of high-gloss paint, reflects light brilliantly, making color seem lighter and more lustrous. A surface with a flat, or matte, finish appears less bright because the finish absorbs rather than reflects the light. Decorative painting techniques such as ragging and sponging produce abstract texture that gives color depth.

The key to working with different textures throughout a room is to introduce enough variety to create interest and modulate color, but not so much that visual chaos results. Try to strike a balance between bland and confusing. If everything in a room is sleek and shiny, for example, offset the smooth, reflective surfaces with a few soft, natural textures.

When you use texture, the scale should correspond to that of the room and its furnishings. Since texture tends to fill space, it's best to use small-scale textures—sparingly—in a small room. Large-scale textures work in a larger room and can even help reduce the apparent size of the room.

Pattern: Pattern enriches decorating schemes by adding movement, depth, and visual interest. It also unifies colors and textures with design. There are no pattern rules. As you choose patterns, look at them alone and in combination.

• **Pattern styles:** Patterns vary in style and size. Naturalistic patterns are realistic renderings of natural forms, such as flowers; they're usually used in formal, traditional settings. Stylized patterns simplify and repeat natural designs; consider the fleur-de-lis, a stylized iris. Use these patterns in both formal and informal decorating schemes.

Abstract patterns are artistic interpretations of realistic designs; large, splashy florals are typical abstract patterns. Geometrics are nonrepresentational designs made up of stripes, plaids, and geometric shapes.

• **Pattern scale:** The size of a design motif when seen in relation to other motifs is referred to as scale. Small-scale or all-over patterns have the softest effect. They're most often used in small rooms where they're clearly seen and the design is retained. When used in larger rooms, some small-scale patterns are so small that they read like a textured surface, an effect you may

A traditional sleigh bed and a building-shaped cupboard are prominent features in this blue- and white-accented room. Patterns of checks and plaids tie together the decor and convey a homey feeling. *Design: Nancy Rubinstein and Jeanne White Interiors*

The fresh, white plate rail and window and door trim contrast crisply with the soft, golden-glazed walls with vine stencils in this simple, country-style setting. *Interior design: Osburn Design Decorative painting: Iris Potter*

want if you're looking for a warm, soft appearance.

To keep a room from seeming too small, choose a pattern with an airy background; your eye will look beyond the pattern, making the room seem more spacious.

Large-scale, multicolored patterns impart a sense of formality and grandeur. Large rooms will support large, brightly colored motifs, even when they appear on dark backgrounds. Because they have the effect of drawing the walls closer, large patterns can consume space and create the impression that the room is smaller than it actually is.

• **Line and pattern:** The lines of an area can suggest the pattern. Subtle vertical stripes visually raise a low cciling or roof. With high ceilings, use random patterns or spreading designs; avoid strong verticals. In an angular room, corners will break the pattern of dominant motifs. A better choice to unify walls is an all-over design with no noticeable repeats.

• **Combining patterns:** Patterns that share at least one color combine easily. Geometric and naturalistic patterns—stripes and florals, for example—are frequently combined. The trick is to unite the patterns with color yet keep distinct contrasts in their designs.

A graceful, traditional decorating scheme gains texture from decorative wall painting, elaborate bed and window curtains and bed linens, and varied accessories.
Interior design: Mark Chastain and Susan Lind Chastain, Fine Custom Sewing
Decorative painting: Spike Lind (ribbons), Barry Nelson and Bill Sandoval (background)

Similar patterns of different scales, such as small checks and larger plaids, also combine well. Again, common colors will help tie the look together.

Don't combine too many patterns. As a rule of thumb, use only one bold pattern on a large surface. Then, add two or possibly three smaller-scale patterns, distributing them around the room to avoid pattern clusters that appear heavy or confusing.

PRINCIPLES OF DESIGN

Although these basic principles deal with intangibles, they're very important when it comes to decorating.
Balance: Design is balanced when a sense of visual equilibrium is achieved. Consider the impact, or visual weight, of each decorative element in the room. Rough textures and bold patterns, for example, increase visual weight and attract attention.

Balance may be symmetrical—the halves are mirror-images—or asymmetrical—equal but not identical visual weights. Symmetrical balance is quiet, restful, and formal. Few areas are purely symmetrical, but elements often are—such as a centered fireplace or identical chairs facing each other.

Asymmetrical balance is active, informal, and more common. With asymmetrical design, visually heavy elements are balanced by less forceful ones placed farther from the area's center. This principle is at work in a pattern that balances visu-

ally heavy motifs with a grouping of lighter ones.

Rhythm: The organized repetition of elements in a design scheme constitutes rhythm. This repetition brings a sense of unity and continuity as the eye moves easily from one motif or area to another. While the repeated elements must share a common trait, such as color, for a sense of unity, they also should be varied to create visual interest.

A geometric wallpaper with a strong repeat design is an example of rhythm. More subtle rhythm comes from repeating the same or similar lines elsewhere in the room.
Emphasis: Emphasis is the principle of making some elements in a design more significant than others. If a painting is a room's focal point, furnishings and wall coverings should be subordinate. A room with no emphasis looks monotonous; too many emphasized elements will vie for your attention.
Scale: When the scale of a wall covering is in proportion to the overall size of the room, the room appears in proportion. With too large a scale, the effect is overpowering; if it's too small, the design will look

weak. You may want to change the perceived size of an area by manipulating scale with pattern *(page 20)*.

Harmony: Harmony results from the presence of both unity and variety. A careful combining of colors, textures, and patterns yields a unified whole. But too much unity can cause a room to look boring and monotonous.

Used properly, variety adds vitality and excitement. It may be subtle, as in slight variations in color, or it may be startling, as with sharply contrasting patterns.

One way to establish harmony is to unify walls and detailings with a common color and vary the surface design from plain to patterned.

DECORATING STYLES

Most home furnishings fall into two broad categories: traditional and contemporary. Traditional styles are linked with the past while contemporary styles represent original statements unconnected to history.

Note, however, that many of the pieces you are likely to find today blend traditional and contemporary elements for a look sometimes called transitional. A heavily carved

antique armoire, for example, may be reproduced with the same basic form but with simplified lines.

Rarely is any area decorated totally in one style or the other. Instead, most people prefer an eclectic style, one that judiciously mixes both the traditional and the contemporary. For example, you can warm up contemporary styles with soft, decorative touches or bring simplicity and lightness to

The eclectic design of this open, colorful den is unified by hues of blue—in the coffee table, couch, wall, wall-hung light fixtures, and bold wall painting.

classic styles. The discussion that follows will offer you a glimpse into the world of traditional and contemporary design.

Traditional: A catch-all term covering many period styles from different cities, regions, and countries, these timeless looks do share some

Representative of the Italian-country style, the rustic kitchen above is marked by copper tile accents and a faux-stone finish for the cabinets, door, ceiling, and walls.
Interior design and decorative painting: Peggy Del Rosario

characteristics: a graceful shape and a formal, quiet order. Whether the details are true antiques or re-creations, continuity with the past is a constant. Rarely, however, are traditional schemes exact re-creations of period styles. Instead, most people usually combine a number of traditional looks, choosing favorite motifs, colors, and patterns from different eras.

Period styles: Among the English periods, 18th-century Georgian produced furniture styles that live on

today—Sheraton, Chippendale, Adam, and Hepplewhite. In French design, elaborate scrollwork and decoration characterized Louis XV pieces; neoclassical Louis XVI furniture featured straight lines and geometric motifs.

Although for the most part the American colonists copied the styles of the English and French, a unique American design tradition emerged. Early American was a simple style based on European design but reinterpreted to reflect a more

This traditionally decorated family room is filled with strong, repeating patterns, textures, and colors. Blue-and-white striped fabric on the walls, ceiling, and couch cushions lend a sense of unity to the area.

Aqua-blue walls and rug accents help unify the stairway, living room, and music room in this open design.

Different stains distinguish the two front gable sections of the adapted version of a traditional colonial house shown above.

The indoor decor reverses things, with the interior of each half painted the color of the other half's exterior *(left)*.

humble lifestyle. Typical designs were stripes and plant motifs.

The Georgian period featured rich hues and scenic wallpapers; consider the furnishings and architecture of Colonial Williamsburg.

Federal, a third American period, was inspired by the neoclassical revival in Europe. Walls were painted plaster or covered with formal, scenic wallpapers from Europe and Asia, and symbols of the eagle and classical motifs were prevalent. Monticello, Thomas Jefferson's home, is one notable example of Federal design.

Romantic: The popularity of the romantic look springs from the renewed interest in the Victorian era. Now regarded as excessive and flamboyant, the Victorian age made one important design contribution: the production of chintz, a popular printed-cotton fabric that was usually glazed. Garden and field supplied the motifs—fruits, flowers, and leaves—in colorful, curved forms. Many of these designs appear today in brighter colors and patterns. Floral wallpaper and fabric capture the whimsy of this style.

Country: The continuing popularity of the country style illustrates the perennial appeal of a simple way of life. It was first defined by hand-hewn furniture, stenciled walls, and antique quilts, reflecting a return to the basics.

Contemporary country is much lighter and less representational. Fewer accessories, larger and more impressionistic patterns, and light wood finishes bring the look up to date.

Two 19th-century styles that ran counter to Victorian excesses now infuse contemporary country with clean, spare design. The first, the Shaker style, is marked by grace and purity. The plain, pared-down Shaker pieces have a timeless quality and hint at the functionality and simplicity of 20th-century design. The second, the Mission or Golden Oak, style is derived from the Craftsman movement. Larger and heavier than Shaker, the sturdy furniture of Gustav Stickley stressed pure joinery and rectilinear design.

Several international styles enjoy the same popularity as American country. English country, with floral chintzes covering overstuffed sofas and chairs in cluttered rooms, was inspired by country houses and cottage gardens. It's a sophisticated, relaxed style. The decorative French country features lively hues and patterns. Humble in origin, its simplicity is reflected in uncontrived pine furniture and colorful Provençal cottons.

Regional: Organic styles such as Southwestern and Mediterranean use colors and forms that harmonize with the environment. Walls are plain rather than patterned; colors range from muted to bright hues drawn from land, sea, and sky. Art and accessories from the most formal regional style, Oriental, lend a romantic exoticism to any setting.

Contemporary: From the curvilinear forms of Art Nouveau to the geometric patterns of Art Deco and the functionality of the Bauhaus movement came contemporary, or modern, interior design. In contrast to traditional designers who copied earlier periods, contemporary designers broke with the past to create a truly original style.

Today the term identifies a spare, strong look that is often called high tech or minimalist. Furniture and exterior details are seen more as form than decoration; brass, glass, chrome, and steel are common materials. A sense of spaciousness is achieved with open, sparse plans, no clutter, and lots of light. The palette may be neutral, pale, or bold, but the color is usually plain. Patterns, if any, tend to be abstract or geometric.

Because it's simple and spare, contemporary is the perfect style to highlight artwork or a beautiful piece of furniture. Mixing in a little old with the new softens the hard-edged effect.

Eclectic: Just as you can blend traditional and contemporary elements for a transitional look, so, too, can you mix distinctly different periods and regions for an eclectic style. For integrated and sophisticated results, you must aim for some sense of order.

One way is to maintain a chosen mood—formal or informal—as you decorate. Repeating a color throughout the room will unify furnishings and accessories. Repeating a pattern will de-emphasize disparate shapes and help create a coordinated look.

One of the benefits of a room decorated in an eclectic style is that everyone feels at home there. And it's the easiest style to add to as you find new pieces or inherit old ones.

Getting the Work Done

Many of us lack the energy, time, or expertise to tackle an interior or exterior home-decorating project from beginning to end. Some jobs you can do yourself; for others, you may require some professional help. For example, you may prefer to do only the unspecialized work, such as applying prepasted wallpaper to a small wall area, but hire experts for everything else. Or, you may decide to tackle all the work yourself. In any case, you need to consider the pros and cons.

DOING THE WORK VERSUS HIRING

To decide whether you can do the job yourself, consider your skills, budget, and available time.

Doing the job: Are you willing and able to paste wallpaper panels all around a room or series of rooms, to sand down rough indoor walls, or to climb a ladder to repair or replace rotted clapboard siding? If so, you can borrow or rent any tools you don't own and do the work yourself. To get a better idea of what's involved in tackling these and other decorating projects, read the instructional material in this book.

Hiring help: The more complicated the job, the more help you're likely to need. If you decide to work only part-time with an expert, consider hiring a general contractor to oversee the tasks with which you are least comfortable. Even if you decide to go it alone, it's still helpful to invite a few contractors to bid on the job. They may offer invaluable input and their bids will help you estimate the potential savings of doing your own work.

DOING IT YOURSELF

If you're ready to tackle the job at hand, consider the following:

Buying materials: Carefully estimate the materials you require, then make a detailed shopping list—if you need help, consult a salesperson. To cut costs, order as many materials as possible at one time. Buy materials in standard dimensions; always purchase 5 to 10 percent more materials than you estimate you'll need to allow for inevitable wastage.

If a contractor is handling part of the job, he may be able to buy materials at a discount. Contractors with large projects nearing completion also are good sources of discount materials, although you may have to make some compromises when it comes to color.

Making a schedule: Think through in advance the exact sequence of procedures. Always be sure to allow for extra time—and money. As well, consider how long you may need to have power and water supplies turned off while work is being done.

CHOOSING A PROFESSIONAL

If you have decided to hire help, be as precise as possible about the look

---

THE PROFESSIONAL CONTRACT

A professional contract binds and protects both you and the professional. Minimize the possibility of misunderstandings later by writing down every possible detail in advance. When acting as your own contractor, agreements with subcontractors should be put into writing. The contract should include all of the following:

• Project and participants: Include a general description of the project, its address, and the names and addresses of both you and all professionals involved.

• Work to be performed: Specify all major jobs—from scraping to finishing.

• Time schedule: The contract should include both start and completion dates. Some contractors will work only at the times you specify. For example, you may want work done only in the morning. Specify this in the contract.

• Method of payment: Payments are usually made in installments as phases of work are completed. It is wiser to insist on a fixed price bid. You also may want to work out an arrangement with a "not-to-

exceed" clause. Stipulate that final payment is withheld until the job receives its final inspection and all liens are cleared.

• Waiver of liens: If subcontractors are not paid for materials or services delivered to your home, in some states they can place a "mechanic's lien" on your property, tying up the title. Protect yourself with a waiver of liens, signed by the general contractor, subcontractors, and major material suppliers. A design store retailer probably will be able to provide you with a copy of a model contract.

Adherence to the elements and principles of good design—including color, texture, and pattern—helps provide a serene mood for this neoclassical living room. An interior designer or decorator can help you achieve the right look.
Interior design and decorative painting: Peggy Del Rosario

or decor that you are hoping for. Collect photographs from magazines, advertisements, and manufacturers' brochures.

It's best to choose a professional who belongs to a trade association—this indicates a willingness to comply with the association's code of ethics. You'll also have an established body that you can turn to if you have any complaints.

To make an informed decision, you'll need to familiarize yourself with the help available. Read on for an introduction to design and construction professionals. Be sure to draw up a contract before starting any work *(opposite).*

Paint contractors: The best place to find a paint contractor is at your local paint dealer. The store manager will have a list of contractors who do residential work in your area. He also will know which companies do the best-quality work and be able to recommend the right one for your needs. If you have the time and want to be extra sure of a top-notch job, you can check the recommended contractor's work by visiting houses he has painted and asking former customers about his work and work habits.

Interior designers or decorators: These professionals provide design expertise and may be able to help with the finishing touches. They specialize in decorating and furnishing rooms, and can offer fresh ideas and advice. Through their contacts, a homeowner has access to materials and products not available at the retail level. Many designers belong to the American Society of Interior Designers (ASID).

Paying an hourly rate may be the simplest arrangement; their advice may be all you need. Other designers charge a percentage of the cost of materials. Friends and neighbors, professional associations, and some retailers can provide good references, if you need them.

Architects: Architects are state-licensed professionals with architecture degrees. They're trained to create designs that are structurally sound, functional, and aesthetically pleasing. If considering major structural changes, these professionals can help prepare plans and a contractor can do the work.

General contractors: Licensed contractors specialize in construction, although some also have design skills. Contractors may do all the work themselves or they may hire subcontractors, order construction materials, and see that the job is completed according to contract.

Get recommendations from friends, architects, and designers, then meet with several contractors. As well, call the Better Business Bureau to find out if there are existing complaints about contractors.

Other specialists: Showroom personnel, home design store salespeople, and other retailers may be all you need to help you create a look that's right for your indoor and outdoor projects. For a larger job, check the specialist's qualifications and references carefully.

Interior PAINTING

Bringing a room to life with a fresh coat of paint is a favorite project among do-it-yourselfers—and no wonder. Interior painting requires only modest expense and effort, yet can yield dramatic results. The following chapter sets out all the information you'll need to complete an interior painting project successfully. Sections on shopping for paint and selecting the right tools contain important information on these first steps in any painting project, while a page on painting safety will help ensure that your work proceeds without any health risks. The chapter also provides step-by-step instructions for making the preparations and repairs commonly needed before painting interior surfaces. A section on painting techniques, along with featured painter's tips and shortcuts, will save you unnecessary time and effort, and help you to get the job done right.

Rich, coppery-brown walls contribute to the elegant look of this living room. The white ceiling, trim, baseboard, and fireplace surround help give the room an open, airy feel.

Shopping for Paint

Although the terminology and profusion of brand names and grades can be overwhelming, a basic understanding of the various types of paint available will go a long way in helping you decide on the right one for the job you're doing.

Different types of paint have their own unique qualities and specific uses. The most common types of paint for interior surfaces are water-base, or latex, and oil-base, or alkyd. Wood stains and clear finishes also are generally available in latex and alkyd formulations. (All these options are discussed in detail on the following pages.)

The chief advantages of higher-quality, generally pricier products, include better hiding (fewer coats required) and better washability.

You must decide on the finish you want for each surface. Latex and alkyd paints are available in a range of finishes, typically from flat to semigloss and gloss. Finish differs among manufacturers, but generally semigloss is halfway between flat and gloss, while eggshell is halfway between flat and semigloss.

Higher-gloss finishes are more washable and durable, but they will show more imperfections in the surface. High-gloss paint is used on trim. Semigloss also is excellent on trim, as well as on kitchen, bathroom, and other surfaces exposed to grease, moisture, and heavy wear. A flat or eggshell finish is best for surfaces that receive less wear, such as living room and bedroom walls and ceilings.

LATEX PAINTS

Latex accounts for the vast majority of house paint sold today, and for good reason. Because it is made with water, latex paint dries quickly, is practically odorless, and poses least threat to the environment. As well, latex paint has excellent resistance to yellowing with age. Best of all, you can clean up latex paint with soap and water.

While today's latex higher-gloss finishes can have better gloss and color retention than alkyd paints, they're not as durable and must be applied over a well cleaned, properly primed surface or they can easily crack or peel.

You can tell latex quality by the type of resin used. The highest quality and most durable latex

How Paint is Changing

The main environmental problem with paint is that it contains thinners, or solvents, which, as they evaporate, release volatile organic compounds into the air. These contribute to smog and can pose health risks. Paint companies have made attempts in recent years to reduce the amount of thinner in their products, replacing it with nonvolatile oil or resin. Modern oil-base paints, made with synthetic resins called alkyds, have less thinner, and give off less odor and toxic fumes. Still, thinner is an essential component of alkyds.

Because the thinner content of latex paint has always been much less than that of alkyd paints, there has been a dramatic shift over the years toward latex. In fact, some oil-base paints are now either restricted or illegal in certain areas. More recently, the already-low solvent content of latex paints (maximum of 7 to 8 percent) has been reduced to zero in some cases. These paints are marked "0 VOC" on the label. While this is good news for the environment, 0 VOC paint is harder to work with because it dries so quickly.

A combination of flat wall paint with high-gloss and faux-marble trim creates a tasteful and refined backdrop for this living room.

Playful colors brighten a child's bedroom and highlight unique decorative elements. Enamel paint was selected because it dries to a hard, easily washable finish that stands up well to wear and tear.

paint contains 100 percent acrylic resin. These paints offer excellent adhesion over alkyds. Low-sheen finishes of 100 percent acrylic are more susceptible to marring, so opt for semigloss. Vinyl acrylic and other blends are next in quality. A latex paint containing solely vinyl resin is the least durable and poorest-quality of the latex formulations

ALKYD PAINTS

Solvent-base paints, made of synthetic resins, have largely replaced paints based on linseed and other natural oils. Alkyds level out better than latexes, drying virtually free of brush marks for a smoother, harder finish. They're a wise choice for glossy surfaces since they offer better adhesion. However, alkyds are harder to apply, tend to sag more, and take longer to dry than latexes. Alkyds also require cleanup with paint thinner. Quality alkyd

paints are made with low-odor mineral spirits so they are more pleasant to apply than regular alkyds. Whenever painting large areas with alkyd paint, ventilate the room or wear a respirator.

ENAMEL PAINTS

The word enamel usually refers to high-gloss paints —alkyd or latex— that dry to a hard finish.

Trim enamel: Apply trim enamel on interior trim.

Polyurethane enamel: Sometimes called liquid-plastic paints, these enamels contain polyurethane and are used for floors because of their high abrasion resistance.

WOOD STAINS

Since most stains are made for a certain effect or condition, it's best to discuss the job with your paint dealer before choosing a product. Pigmented, or dye-colored, wiping

stain is one of the most commonly used. You simply apply the stain, wait a while, and wipe it off. If the surface feels rough, apply a clear, quick-drying sanding sealer, then sand it smooth.

CLEAR FINISHES

If you want to display the grain of wood that is bare or has been stained, choose polyurethane, varnish, shellac, or one of several clear, nonyellowing water-base coatings available. Most come in a range of finishes from flat to gloss.

Polyurethane: Apply polyurethane to cabinets and wood paneling when maximum durability is required.

Varnish: While durable, varnishes aren't as tough as polyurethane. Ask your paint dealer for the best type for your job. Thin and clean up with paint thinner.

Shellac: Apply shellac, which comes in orange or white, only over bare

ESTIMATING PAINT NEEDS

To figure out how much paint you'll need, you must know the square footage of the area you intend to paint and the spread rate of the paint (spread rate usually is about 400 square feet to the gallon, but check the can you buy to be sure).

To determine the square footage, measure the width of each wall, add the figures together, and multiply the total by the room's height.

Next, estimate how much of this area contains surfaces that won't be painted, such as a fireplace, windows, wallpaper, and areas you'll paint separately, such as trim. If these surfaces account for 10 percent or more of the room, deduct the amount from the total.

Finally, to figure out how many gallons of paint you'll need, divide the square footage by the spread rate of the paint. You can calculate the amount of trim paint separately. Or, like professional painters, you can figure on about a quarter as much trim paint as wall paint.

A chair-rail molding creates a natural border for contrasting wall colors. Off-white window trim, baseboards, and curtains soften the effect and tie the elements together.

or stained wood. It isn't suggested for areas exposed to moisture; water causes spotting on the finish. Most brush marks that appear in wet shellac aren't visible when the shellac has dried. Use denatured alcohol for thinning and cleaning up.

Water-base transparent coating: Some transparent coatings, including nonyellowing types, can be used on bare or stained wood as well as on painted surfaces, specifically to protect decorative latexes. For more information, see page 63.

PRIMERS

You need a primer when the surface to be painted is porous or the paints are incompatible (such as when you apply latex over alkyd). An existing painted surface in good condition and compatible with the finish coat may not need an additional primer. Consult the chart on the opposite page to determine if a primer is required. If you need more information, ask your dealer.

Indoor Painting Safety

Although paint is fairly user-friendly, it's best to exercise caution when working with it. Listed here are some basic safety guidelines.

• Carefully read the labels on paint cans for warnings about possible hazards and heed all safety instructions provided.

• Keep paint products out of reach of children.

• Always work with paint products in an area that is well ventilated. Open doors and windows, and use exhaust fans. Excessive inhalation of fumes from paints and solvents can cause dizziness, headache, fatigue, and nausea. Also, keep pets out of freshly painted rooms. Paint fumes are especially dangerous to pet birds.

• If you can't ventilate the area well enough to get rid of the fumes, wear an approved respirator (a type of mask that will filter vapors). Respirators are available at paint and hardware stores.

• Wear a dust mask and safety goggles when you're sanding to keep from breathing in dust particles and to protect your eyes.

• Wear safety goggles to protect your eyes from splashes when using chemical strippers or caustic cleaning compounds, or when painting overhead.

• Use canvas drop cloths on the floor. Cloth stays in place and won't be as slippery as plastic.

• Don't use or store paint products near a flame or heat source. Avoid smoking while painting or while using thinner.

• Many paints and solvents are particularly harmful to the skin and eyes. Be especially careful when handling or applying products that contain strong solvents; again, read the labels. Wear gloves and a respirator when necessary. Also, wear gloves when applying paint with a sponge or rag.

• Inspect ladders for sturdiness. Make sure that all four legs rest squarely on the floor and both cross braces are locked in place. Never stand on the top step or on the utility shelf. Never lean away from a ladder. Instead, get off and move the ladder if you can't reach a spot easily.

• For scaffolding planks, use 2-by-10s no more than 12 feet long. If you place the planks between two ladders, position the ladders so their steps are facing each other. If you run planks between ladders or a ladder and sawhorse or stairway step, be sure the planks are level.

• Clean up promptly after painting and properly dispose of soiled rags; check local codes for disposal regulations. Spread rags soaked with alkyd paint or paint thinner outdoors and let them dry all day before throwing them in the trash. Don't leave rags to dry in areas accessed by children or pets.

INTERIOR PAINTS FOR ALL SURFACES

SURFACE	PRIME OR FIRST COAT	FINISH COAT(S)	COMMENTS
New wallboard	Prime with latex sealer and let dry at least 4 hours.	Apply two coats of latex or alkyd paint in finish of choice. Sand lightly between coats of eggshell, semigloss, or gloss alkyd paint.	Don't use alkyd primer—it will raise nap in paper.
New plaster	Prime with latex sealer and let dry at least 4 hours.	Apply two coats of latex or alkyd paint in finish of choice. Sand lightly between coats of eggshell, semigloss, or gloss alkyd paint.	None.
Existing wallboard or plaster	When painting over existing latex paint, scuff sand to remove surface imperfections. If surface is dirty, wash and rinse thoroughly first.	Apply two coats of latex or alkyd paint in finish of choice. Sand lightly between coats of eggshell, semigloss, or gloss alkyd paint.	To test if existing paint is alkyd or latex, apply nail polish remover to a small section. Latex will dissolve; alkyd won't.
Bare wood to be painted	Use an alkyd enamel undercoat.	Lightly sand enamel undercoat and apply two coats of finish paint.	Minimum sheen for woodwork is eggshell. Semigloss is preferable on doors and trim.
Painted wood to be repainted	Remove loose, flaking paint and sand smooth. Spot-prime bare wood with alkyd enamel undercoat.	Apply a first coat of latex or alkyd enamel paint; let dry thoroughly. Sand lightly, then apply a second coat and allow to dry overnight.	Minimum sheen for woodwork is eggshell. Semigloss is preferable on doors and trim.
Bare wood to be stained	Sand wood smooth. Apply a single coat of interior wiping stain and allow to dry overnight. For open-grain woods such as oak and mahogany, stain can be mixed 1:1 with paste wood filler to stain and fill grain in one application.	Apply one coat of varnish and allow to dry overnight. Sand lightly with steel wool or fine sandpaper. Apply at least three more coats, with overnight drying and sanding between coats.	Don't apply polyurethane over shellac or sanding sealers since adhesion problems can result.
Bare wood to be coated with a clear finish	Apply varnish, polyurethane, or other clear finish in desired sheen.	Apply two or three additional coats of clear finish, sanding between coats.	Don't apply polyurethane over shellac or sanding sealers since adhesion problems can result.
Masonry	On new block, use latex block filler. On poured concrete or brick, prime with latex sealer.	Apply two coats of latex finish.	White, powdery residue (efflorescence) is a sign of moisture in masonry. Check exterior walls for drainage problems and make any needed repairs.
Metal	Remove rust with wire brush. Prime steel with rust-inhibitive primer. Prime aluminum or galvanized metal with galvanized metal primer.	Apply two coats of finish paint.	Flat finish paint isn't recommended.

Selecting the Right Tools

Good-quality tools suited to the task and used the right way will go a long way in assuring you achieve a professional-looking paint job.

For most painting projects, at least several high-quality brushes and a good roller are essential.

PAINTBRUSHES

Natural-bristle brushes are traditionally used to apply alkyd paint and other finishes that require paint thinner for cleaning. Avoid using these brushes for applying latex paint and other water-base products because the bristles become limp when they soak up water.

You can get by nicely with three brushes: a 2-inch trim brush, a 1½-inch angled sash brush, and a 4-inch straight-edged brush. Good-quality brushes perform very differently from less expensive ones. They have long, flagged bristles set firmly into a wooden handle with epoxy cement, not glue. A good brush is well balanced, holds a lot of paint, and puts the paint where you want it. Inspect any brush carefully before you buy it. Grip it as if you were painting. It should feel comfortable in your hand—not awkward or heavy. Fan out the bristles and check for flagged, or split, ends. The more of these there are, the more paint the brush can hold.

INTERIOR PAINTING TOOLS

In addition to brushes, rollers, and other paint applicators, tools needed for interior painting often include items used in preparing surfaces, such as a scraper, sanding block, and putty knife.

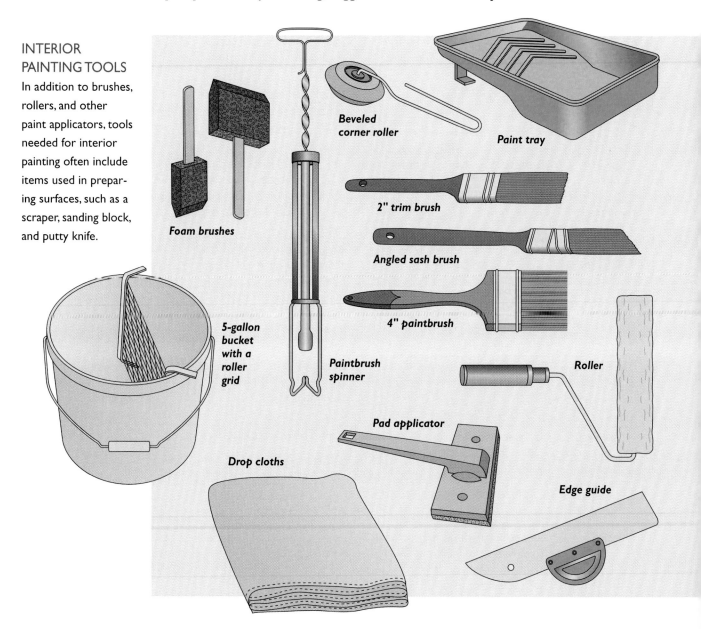

Foam brushes

Beveled corner roller

Paint tray

2" trim brush

Angled sash brush

4" paintbrush

5-gallon bucket with a roller grid

Paintbrush spinner

Roller

Pad applicator

Drop cloths

Edge guide

Most of the bristles should be long, but there should be a few short bristles mixed in. The bristles should be thick, flexible, and tapered so that they're thicker at the base than at the tip.

PAINT ROLLERS

Look for a roller with a heavy-gauge steel frame, an expandable wire sleeve, a good-quality cover, or nap, and a comfortable handle threaded with a metal sleeve to accommodate an extension pole. A 9-inch roller will handle nearly all jobs. For some work, you may prefer a special roller: a trim roller for painting trim and window sashes; a beveled corner roller for corners, ceiling borders, and grooves in paneling; and a roller made of grooved foam for acoustical surfaces.

When buying a roller, choose the right nap for the paint you're using.

With latex, you'll want a nylon nap. Nylon and wool blend, lambskin, and mohair covers are recommended for alkyd paint. Nap thickness varies from $1/16$ inch to $1^1/4$ inches. The smoother the surface that you're painting and the higher the gloss of paint that you're applying, the shorter the nap you'll need.

A 3- to 4-foot-long extension pole allows you to reach high walls and ceilings, in many cases eliminating the need for ladders or scaffolding. Use the extension pole when painting low areas to avoid stooping.

For bigger jobs, rolling from a 5-gallon bucket equipped with a roller grid is faster and neater than using a roller tray. Don't bother with a roller shield, a device intended to minimize spattering. Spatter is due to excessive speed in rolling and to improper roller nap thickness. Inexpensive paints also tend to spatter more.

OTHER PAINT APPLICATORS

Disposable foam brushes are sometimes handy for small jobs and quick touchups. A pad applicator with a replaceable pad is useful for painting corners and edges. As with roller covers made of the same materials, nylon pads are used with latex paints; nylon and wool blend, lambskin, and mohair pads are recommended for alkyd paints.

A painter's mitt is ideal for painting irregular or contoured surfaces, such as pipes, grilles, and radiators. You dip the mitt into the paint and rub the paint onto the surface. This technique is shown on page 185.

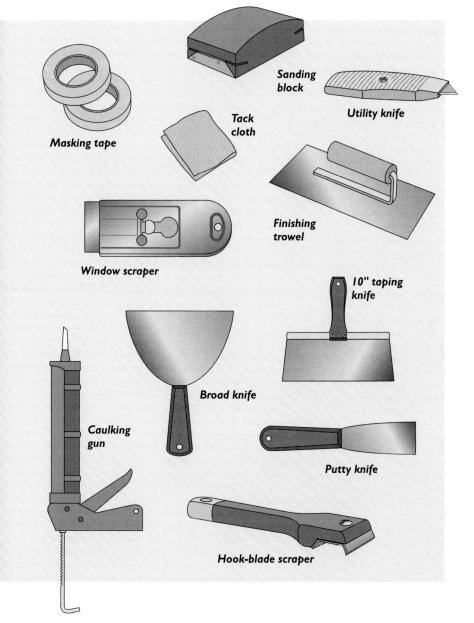

Masking tape

Sanding block

Tack cloth

Utility knife

Window scraper

Finishing trowel

10" taping knife

Broad knife

Caulking gun

Putty knife

Hook-blade scraper

Preparing Surfaces for Painting

Before you start painting, you'll need to do some preparation work. In some cases, it also will be necessary to make repairs to wall surfaces. For detailed information on repairing surfaces, see pages 42 to 47.

ORGANIZING THE ROOM

Move light furniture pieces and accessories out of the room. Push heavy furniture into the middle of the room and cover it with drop cloths. Remove everything you can from the walls.

Unscrew heating- and cooling-system duct covers. After turning off the power to the room, remove electrical faceplates and any fixtures. If you can't take down a light fixture, tie a plastic garbage bag around it as shown on page 55. It's best to remove knobs, handles, and locks from doors and windows. Mark all pieces so you can replace them correctly later.

Protect the flooring with canvas drop cloths, which, unlike plastic sheeting, absorb paint. Use masking tape to protect edges of adjacent surfaces (see opposite page).

SCRAPING

Chipped or peeling paint must be scraped off interior surfaces before new paint is applied. The trick is to scrape hard enough to remove the paint, but not so hard that you dig into the surface. The best scrapers have edges that can be sharpened with a metal file. A broad knife does a fast job on large areas; a hook-blade scraper is more convenient for small areas. A wire brush is effective for removing light flaking.

Sometimes the old finish is in such bad condition that the paint must be removed entirely. The easiest way to strip old paint is with a commercial liquid paint stripper. Follow the application directions on the container.

Although you can sometimes paint over wallpaper, it's usually a good idea to remove it, especially if it's tearing or flaking. For information on removing wallpaper, see page 98. After all the adhesive is removed, wash the wall with an abrasive cleaner, rinse well, and let the surface dry for 24 hours.

SANDING

One reason to sand a surface is to smooth it. Walls that you have scraped should then be sanded lightly before painting. You also need to sand newly patched areas and roughen bare wood before beginning to paint.

Another reason to sand is to rough up glossy surfaces before painting. This gives the finish "bite" so the new paint will adhere better. You can use sandpaper on both latex and alkyd paints. Liquid deglosser or trisodium phosphate (TSP) also can be used on alkyds.

If you're using sandpaper on a surface with a very high sheen, begin sanding with coarse-grade sandpaper and finish the job with fine-grade sandpaper. A liquid deglosser is convenient for hard-to-sand areas as well as for remov-

Dealing with Lead-base Paint

Long known as a health hazard, lead paint was phased out of use in the U.S. by 1978. If your house predates the late 1970's, however, layers of lead paint may be hiding under your current finish. While lead paint poses no threat when covered and left untouched, once you start sanding, as when preparing a surface for painting, lead dust will be released into the air, posing significant health risks—especially for young children and pregnant women.

If you suspect your house may contain lead paint, call the National Lead Clearinghouse (NLC) at 1-888-424-5323. Experts there can tell you where to send a paint chip for analysis. In cases where the lead level is low, you can remove the paint yourself so long as you take the recommended precautions. Otherwise, you will be advised to hire professionals to deal with the problem. The use of lead-paint test kits is not recommended by the NLC.

ing floor wax from baseboards. TSP acts as a deglosser, but only where a light sanding is needed. To protect you hands, wear rubber gloves when using a liquid deglosser or TSP. Rinse the wall thoroughly afterwards.

CLEANING

After vacuuming the room, use a tack cloth to dust all the surfaces that will be painted. Then, wash walls that have a grease film (kitchens) or a soap film (bathrooms) with TSP. Greasy or mildewed surfaces should be washed both before and after you sand to prevent impurities from being forced into the surface dur-

ing sanding. For very greasy spots, sponge on paint thinner, blot dry, and wash with the cleaner. In mildewed areas, it's not enough to simply wash the surface. To kill the mildew spores, scrub the walls with liquid bleach or with a solution of half bleach and half water. Follow up by washing with TSP. Allow all washed surfaces to dry thoroughly (about 24 hours).

Periodic cleaning of painted surfaces with water and a mild detergent can reduce the need for frequent repainting.

MASKING

If you have a steady hand, you may not need masking tape to protect

hardware and surfaces next to those being painted. However, most people find tape helpful for keeping surfaces from being splattered and for keeping a crisp edge between two types or colors of paint.

It's important to have the right masking tape. If you're using a brush against the tape, use tape with good adhesion for a tight edge rather than all-purpose tape. That way, you won't have a problem with paint seeping behind the tape. There is a type of tape (often called painter's tape) that can be fastened to delicate surfaces such as wallpaper and won't cause damage when it is pulled away.

Applying masking tape

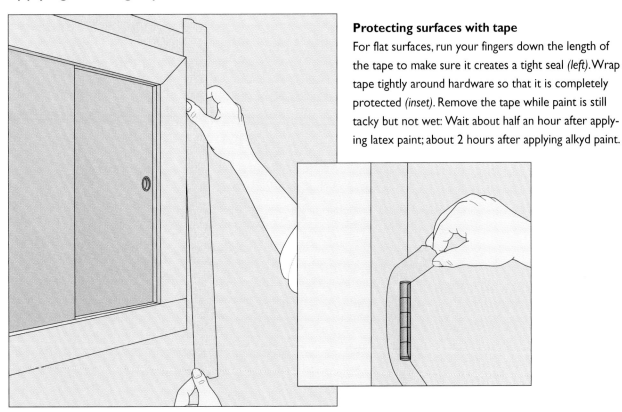

Protecting surfaces with tape
For flat surfaces, run your fingers down the length of the tape to make sure it creates a tight seal *(left)*. Wrap tape tightly around hardware so that it is completely protected *(inset)*. Remove the tape while paint is still tacky but not wet: Wait about half an hour after applying latex paint; about 2 hours after applying alkyd paint.

Repairing Damaged Surfaces

Inspect the area you're painting for holes, cracks, and other minor surface damage. You can make most repairs yourself, although you may have to call in a professional for extensive damage. Large cracks may indicate uneven settling of the house. If you can fit the tip of your little finger into a crack, consider having your foundation inspected.

After you have made a surface repair, you likely will need to sand the surface, and in most cases you will have to apply a primer to ensure that the repair won't show.

Patching a hole in plaster over lath

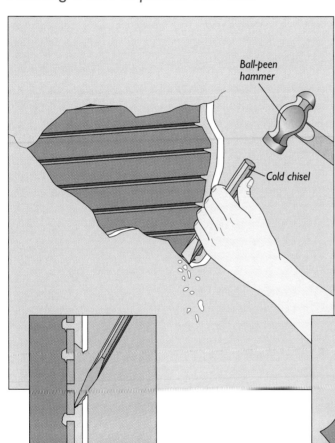

Ball-peen hammer

Cold chisel

Patching compound

6" knife

1 Preparing the area
Remove cracked plaster from the edges with a cold chisel and a ball-peen hammer *(left)*. Undercut the edges *(inset)* to ensure a good bond and brush or blow away debris. Dampen the edges with a sponge.

2 Applying the first patching coat
Using a 6-inch broad knife, fill about half the hole's depth with patching compound, forcing it through the gaps in the lath *(right)*. Score the patch with a nail *(page 45)* to provide "bite" for the next coat, then allow the patch to dry.

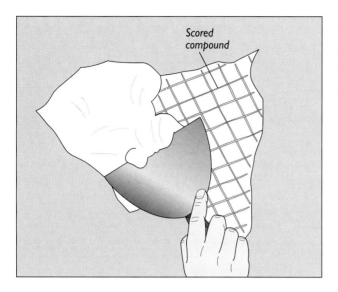

Scored compound

3 Applying the second coat

Moisten the patch again, then apply a second layer of patching compound to within $1/8$ to $1/4$ inch of the surface *(left)*. Score the patch and let it dry.

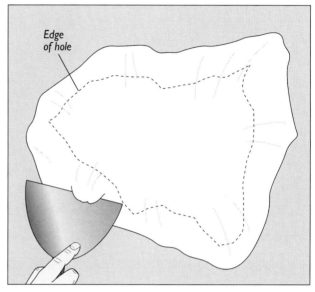

Edge of hole

4 Applying the finishing layer

Use a broad knife to apply a finishing coat, feathering the edges an inch or so beyond the edges of the hole *(right)*.

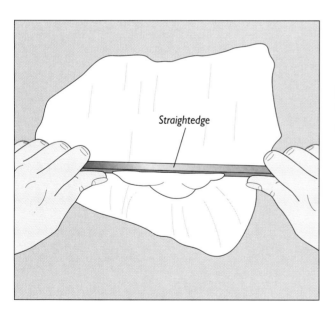

Straightedge

5 Striking off the finishing coat

Strike off the wet finishing coat with a straightedge to remove the excess *(left)*.

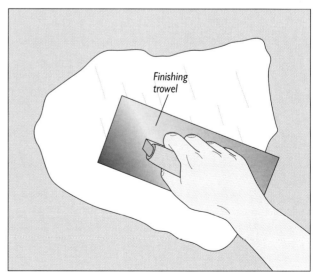

Finishing trowel

6 Smoothing the patch

For a smooth finish, dip a finishing trowel in water and, holding the trowel at a slight angle to the wall, draw it down from top to bottom *(right)*. When the patch is dry, sand and prime.

Patching an open hole

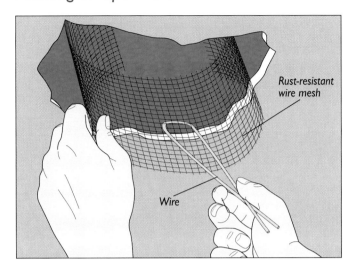

Rust-resistant
wire mesh

Wire

1 Inserting the mesh
After removing loose bits at the hole edges with a cold chisel and a ball-peen hammer *(Step 1, page 42),* loop a length of wire through a section of rust-resistant metal mesh *(left)* and insert the mesh into the hole. Wind the ends of the wire tightly around a stick, pulling the mesh against the hole's back edges.

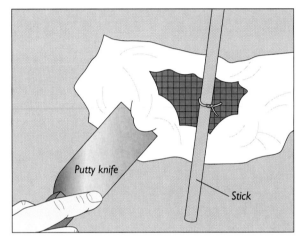

2 Filling the hole
Dampen the edges of the hole with a sponge. Using a putty knife, force patching compound through the mesh *(right)* and fill about half the hole's depth. Score the patch to provide "bite" for the next layer. When the compound is firm, unwind the wire and remove the stick. Complete the patch as described on page 43.

Putty knife

Stick

Filling a small crack

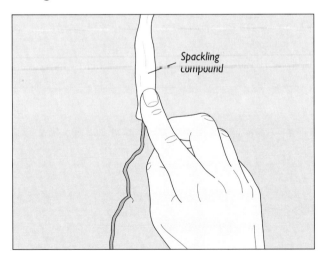

Spackling
compound

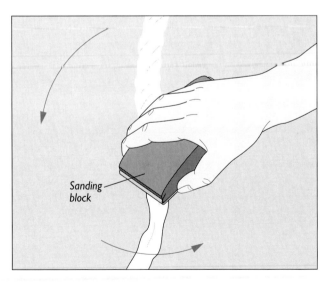

Sanding
block

1 Filling the crack
Widen the crack to about $\frac{1}{8}$ inch with a cold chisel and blow out the dust. Use your finger or a putty knife to fill the crack with spackling compound; let dry. If you use your finger, don't press too hard or the repaired surface will be concave.

2 Finishing the patch
With a sanding block and fine-grade sandpaper, sand the filled crack in a circular motion until smooth. Prime with sealer before painting.

Patching a wide crack

1 Filling the crack

Undercut the crack with the tip of a cold chisel or a putty knife to help the patch bond, then brush or blow out dust and debris. Dampen the crack with a wet paintbrush or sponge. Using a putty knife, apply the first layer of patching compound (right), which should fill a little more than half the depth, leaving space for two more layers. Let each layer dry completely before adding the next. Score the first two layers of plaster with a nail when firm but not hard (inset). This will provide "bite" for the next layer.

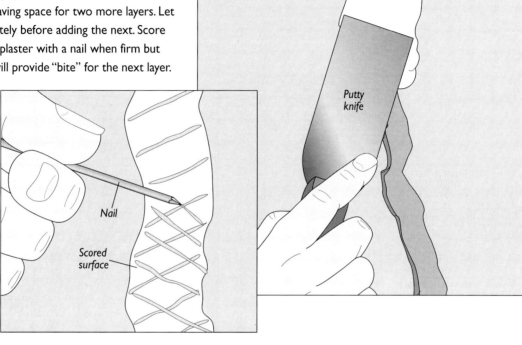

Patching compound

Putty knife

Nail

Scored surface

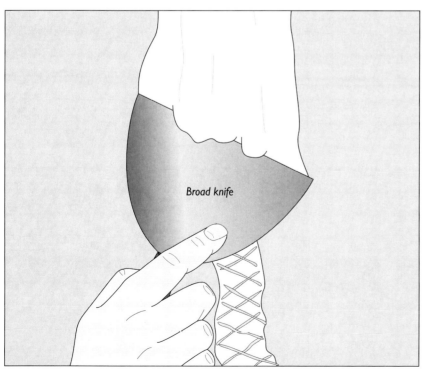

Broad knife

2 Completing the patch

Wet the patch again, then use a 6-inch broad knife to apply the next layer to within $1/8$ to $1/4$ inch of the surface (left). Let the patch dry before adding the finish coat, striking off and smoothing the patch as shown on page 43.

Repairing a large hole in wallboard

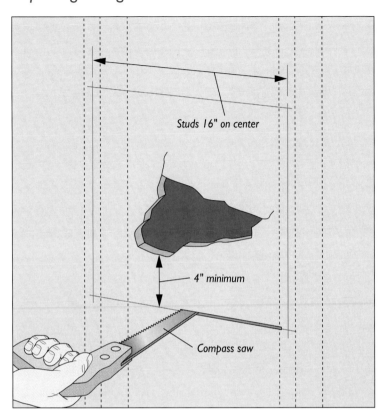

Studs 16" on center

4" minimum

Compass saw

1 Removing a damaged section
Cut away the wallboard to the nearest stud on each side of the hole. (If necessary, locate the wall studs with a commercial stud finder or probe behind the wall with a wire.) Use a compass saw to make horizontal cuts above and below the hole *(left)*, then cut the sides and corners with a utility knife (center the side cuts over the studs). Beware of any wiring or plumbing inside walls. Pry out the damaged wallboard and remove any remaining nails or screws. Note: If you will be installing a commercial patch with adhesive-backed "fins," enlarge the opening to the size of the patch.

2 Attaching a new piece
Cut a replacement piece as thick as the original to size, then smooth rough edges with a perforated rasp. Screw or nail the new piece to the studs. Load about half the blade of a 6-inch broad knife with joint compound. Apply the compound to the joints and then draw the knife along the joints at a 45° angle *(right)*. Note: To repair a bathroom wall, you may be using water-resistant wallboard. Finish this type of wallboard with water-resistant compound following the manufacturer's instructions.

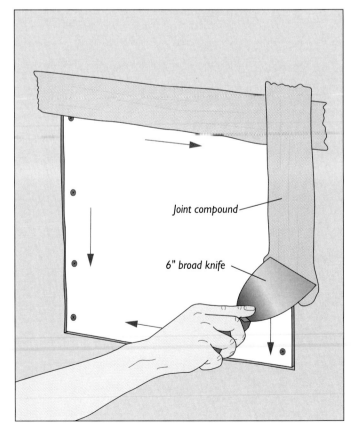

Joint compound

6" broad knife

3 Taping the joints

This step blends the repair with the surrounding surface and is staggered over several days. Center strips of 2-inch joint tape over each joint and press the tape down with a 6-inch broad knife (right). Remove excess joint compound with the knife; feather the edges. Thinly apply compound over the tape. Let the compound dry for at least 24 hours. When dry, wet the patch with a sponge and sand the compound using No. 600 silicone-carbide sandpaper on a sanding block. Don't sand the wallboard paper—the scratches may show through the finish. Apply a second coat of compound and feather the edges. When the compound is dry, wet-sand the edges to remove minor imperfections. Caution: When sanding, wear safety goggles and a dust mask.

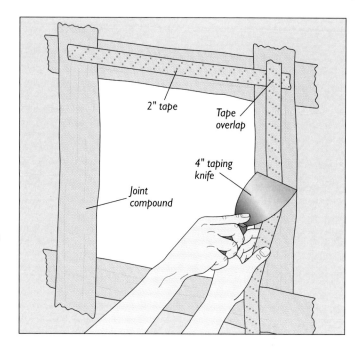

2" tape

Tape overlap

4" taping knife

Joint compound

10" taping knife

4 Applying the third coat of compound

Apply a third layer of compound, using a 10-inch taping knife held at a 45° angle to the wall (left). Use only as much compound as needed to cover the previous layer.

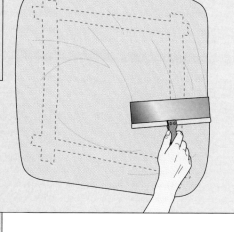

5 Feathering the edges

Using a 10" taping knife, feather the edges of the third coat by 12 to 18 inches (left). Try to level and smooth any ridges in the compound. Allow the compound to dry before doing the final sanding.

Sanding block

6 Wet-sanding and finishing

Give the compound a final wet-sanding to remove imperfections (left). Wipe off sanding residue with a wet sponge and allow the compound to dry. Then, apply a primer or base coat of paint or, for wallpaper, seal the repair with shellac or varnish.

Painting Techniques

The best way to avoid painting yourself into a corner, splattering paint onto newly painted surfaces, or inadvertently touching a just-painted edge is to follow a painting sequence. If you are using stains or clear finishes on woodwork, apply them first. Next, paint the ceiling. Then, paint the walls, starting from the top and working your way down. Finally, brush paint on trim—first the moldings and then the windows, doors, and cabinets.

When you apply two coats of glossy paint, as is often the case when you paint trim, ensure a good bond by sanding lightly between coats and wiping with a tack cloth. Rollers cover walls much faster and more easily than brushes. But professionals sometimes use brushes for walls because they produce a smoother, less porous finish. Use a brush to "cut in" borders around areas that will be rolled *(page 50)* and to paint trim. Avoid painting directly from the can; instead, pour the paint into a larger bucket. You may want to "box" the paint—that is, mix paint from two or more cans to eliminate slight color differences among cans.

When you're working overhead, carry less paint on your brush or roller, and wear a hat and safety goggles for splatter protection. For more information on painting techniques, see Chapter 6, Exterior Painting *(pages 146-188)*.

Painting with a brush

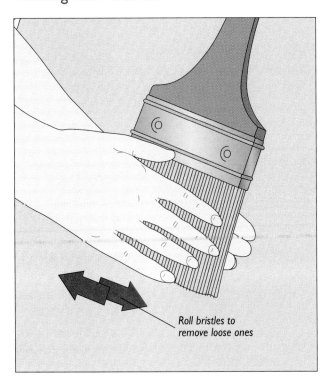

Roll bristles to remove loose ones

1 Removing loose bristles
Before starting, roll the bristles between your palms to remove any loose bristles *(left)*, then shake the brush vigorously. If you moisten the bristles first (use water for latex paint, paint thinner for alkyd), be sure to wipe off any excess moisture to prevent drips when you begin painting.

Stir gently to spread bristles

2 Stirring paint to spread bristles
Half fill a clean, rimless bucket with paint that has been stirred. Dip the brush one-third the length of its bristles into the paint and stir gently to saturate the bristles.

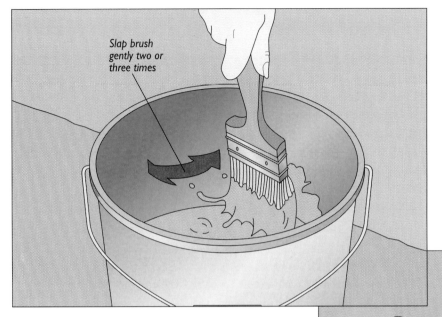

Slap brush gently two or three times

3 Removing excess paint

Lift the brush straight up, letting excess paint drip into the bucket. Gently slap both sides of the brush against the inside of the bucket two or three times *(left)*. Don't wipe the brush across the lip of the bucket or the bristles may separate into clumps, leaving too little paint on the brush.

4 Spreading paint

Spread paint smoothly and evenly on a 3-foot area, gradually reducing pressure at the end of the stroke. Paint from a dry area to a wet edge *(right)*. On smooth surfaces, direct the final strokes one way; on rough surfaces, vary the direction; and on wood, paint parallel to the grain.

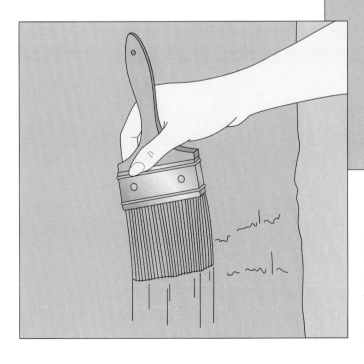

5 Blending brush marks

When the first 3-foot area is filled, blend the brush marks by running the unloaded brush very lightly over the wet paint *(left)*. Begin the next area a few inches away from last finished area. When new area is completed, brush into previously finished area, blending the overlap.

CUTTING IN WITH A BRUSH

Cutting in is the technique of painting with a brush along the edges and corners of a surface, and around any fixtures or trim. The rest of the surface is filled in later (usually with a paint roller, but a brush may be preferable in some cases).

With latex paint, you can cut in the entire room before painting the open spaces. With alkyd paints or deep colors, however, cut in one section at a time and then complete this area before moving on to the next. This is done because the cut-in area has a working time of about only 20 minutes; after that, the overlapped areas will look inconsistent when they have dried.

Cut in first where the ceiling meets the wall. If you're using the same color and type of paint for the ceiling and wall, you can paint the joint and several inches out on both sides. If you're using a different color or type of paint on the ceiling, cut in and roll the ceiling before you paint the walls.

Cutting in with a brush

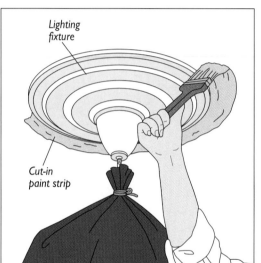

Lighting fixture

Cut-in paint strip

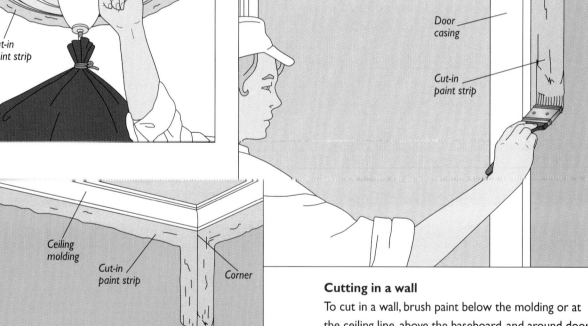

Door casing

Cut-in paint strip

Ceiling molding

Cut-in paint strip

Corner

Cutting in a ceiling
To cut in a ceiling, brush on paint above the molding or at the ceiling line and around any light fixtures (*left*).

Cutting in a wall
To cut in a wall, brush paint below the molding or at the ceiling line, above the baseboard, and around door (*above*) and window frames. You can also cut in by painting against the bristles; see page 185.

Cutting in a corner
In a corner (*left*), use a brush to paint the joint and a 2-inch or wider strip on each side of it.

Painting with a roller

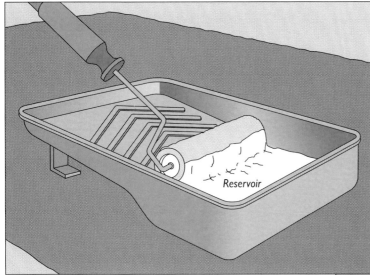

Reservoir

Run roller over grid

5-gallon bucket

1 Loading the roller
You can paint from either a roller tray or a 5-gallon bucket depending on the size of the job. If you're using a tray, pour just enough paint to fill the reservoir end. Dip the roller into the reservoir, then roll up and down the textured part of the tray to distribute paint and saturate the nap (above). In both cases, the roller should be full but not dripping when lifted. For larger jobs, pour 1 or 2 gallons of paint into a 5-gallon bucket and dip in the roller. To distribute paint on the roller, run it back and forth on a grid positioned in the bucket (right).

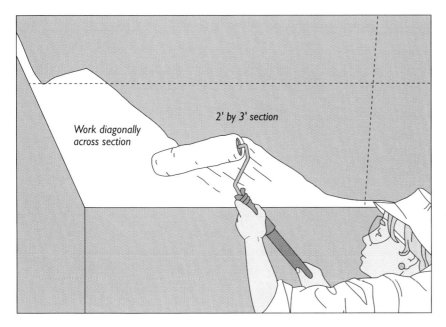

Work diagonally across section

2' by 3' section

2 Rolling the ceiling
Paint the ceiling first. Do a small section (about 2 feet by 3 feet) at a time, starting in a corner and going across the ceiling's shorter dimension. Apply paint diagonally, then roll back and forth to distribute it evenly over the area. Reload the roller often and roll slowly to avoid splattering.

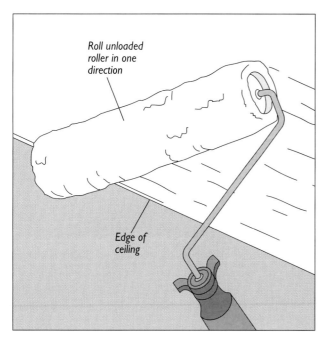

Roll unloaded roller in one direction

Edge of ceiling

3 Rolling the edge of the ceiling

Roll as close to the edges of the ceiling as possible to cover any differences in texture between brush marks made when cutting in and the roller marks. For the final strokes on the ceiling, lightly roll the unloaded roller across each section in one direction.

4 Rolling the walls

Next, roll the walls. Starting in an upper corner of one wall and working from top to bottom, apply paint thickly in a series of big Ws (right). Then, go back over the area, rolling in different directions to fill in the W. Roll slowly to avoid splattering.

Roll big Ws on wall

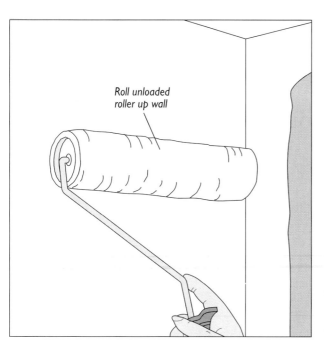

Roll unloaded roller up wall

5 Rolling close to edges and corners

Apply paint with a roller close to edges and corners to conceal the differences between brush marks made when cutting in and roller marks. Finish by rolling the unloaded roller up the wall in one direction, working from bottom to top (left).

Whether you paint a door on or off its hinges, the painting sequence is exactly the same.

To remove a door from its opening, slip the hinge pins out, but don't unscrew the hinges. Lean the door against a wall with two small blocks under the bottom edge and a third wedge between the top edge and the wall. You also can lay the door across a pair of sawhorses; don't apply too much paint, though, or it may puddle.

Paint doors from top to bottom. For flat doors, roll on the paint, then brush it out in the direction of the grain. For doors with inset panels, follow the sequence shown below. Match the color of the latch edge to the room the door opens into and the color of the hinge edge to the room the door opens away from.

When painting the door casing, begin with the head casing and work down the side casings. If the door opens away from the room, paint the jamb and the two surfaces of the door stop visible from the room. If the door opens into the room, paint the jamb and the door side of the door stop. Don't rehang or close the door until all the paint is completely dry.

Painting doors

Panel molding

Panel

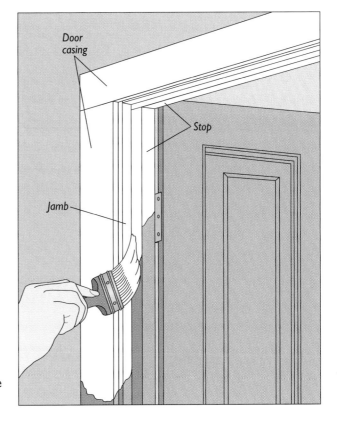

Painting a door with inset panels
On a door with inset panels *(left)*, paint sections in the following order: panel moldings, recesses, panels, strips horizontal then vertical.

Door casing

Stop

Jamb

Painting door jambs and stops
If the door opens away from a room, paint the jamb and two surfaces of the stop as shown at right. If the door opens into the room, paint the jamb and the door side of the stop.

PAINTING WINDOWS

When painting windows, the right brush is important. Choose an angled sash brush; it will reach into corners. Load the brush lightly.

If you don't have a steady hand, you may want to cover the edges of the glass with masking tape to shield them. See page 41 for information on masking. (For techniques on removing paint from window panes, see page 58.) Don't leave tape on windows in the sun too long since it may bond to the glass.

Let the paint slightly overlap the glass. This will seal the finish to the glass so that condensation forming on the glass won't get under the paint and cause it to peel.

Double-hung windows: If the sashes are removable, lift them out, lay them on a table, and paint them. Be prepared to leave the sashes out long enough to dry thoroughly. If the sashes aren't removable, you'll need to raise and lower them as needed to reach all window parts.

Paint the outer, or upper, sash first. If the window has small glass panes, begin with the horizontal muntins and then work on the vertical ones. Next, paint the exposed parts of the stiles, the top rail, and the bottom rail, in that order. Then, paint the inner, or lower, sash, starting with the muntins and finishing with the rails.

To paint the trim of a double-hung window, begin with the head casing, then paint down the sides. Next, paint the stool, then finish with the apron.

Casement windows: First, paint any vertical muntins and then any horizontal ones. Next, paint the top rails, the bottom rails, and the stiles, in that order. Finish the job by painting the casing.

No matter what type of window you have, don't paint the jamb. This may cause the window to stick to it later. Once the window is painted, wax the jamb with floor wax if it is made from wood. You don't need to wax a metal jamb.

ANATOMY OF A DOUBLE-HUNG WINDOW

The interior elements of a double-hung window that must be painted are shown at right. Follow the order recommended above. Casement windows have similar basic parts, but they open differently, swinging outward rather than sliding up and down.

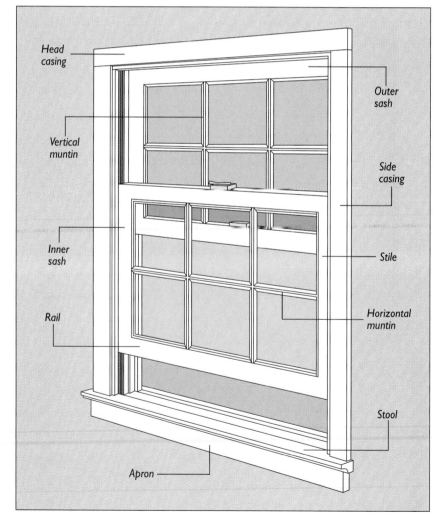

Head casing

Outer sash

Vertical muntin

Side casing

Inner sash

Stile

Rail

Horizontal muntin

Stool

Apron

Painting Tricks and Shortcuts

The following tips from professional painters will help you do a top-quality job yourself.

• For best adhesion when using alkyd enamels and polyurethane varnishes, apply all coats within 72 hours of each other.

• To avoid having to clean your paint tray, line the inside with aluminum foil or plastic. When the job is done, simply remove the liner.

• To remove bristles that come off as you apply paint, touch them with the tip of your wet brush; the bristles should stick to it. Wipe the stray bristles off the brush with a cloth.

• If insects get trapped in the wet paint, let the paint dry before brushing them off.

• When applying an enamel finish coat, brush paint on generously and use a light touch. Avoid over-brushing when you use enamel since it can produce an irregular finish. It's important to work quickly and not try to touch up areas you've already painted.

• If you're sensitive to the odor of paint, mix in a few drops of vanilla extract or add a commercial paint-fragrance additive. However, always wear a respirator if you can't properly ventilate the room.

More tricks and shortcuts

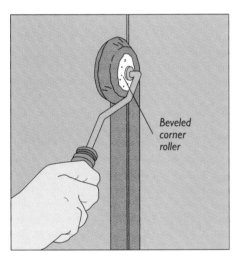

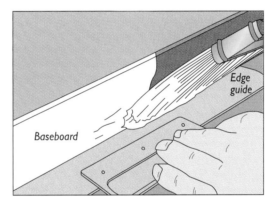

Using a flexible edge guide

A flexible edge guide allows you to paint a baseboard below the carpet line without getting paint on the carpet. Push the guide and your brush in tandem along the baseboard (left).

Using a beveled corner roller
A beveled corner roller is designed to spread paint evenly in corners, avoiding paint buildup in recesses (above).

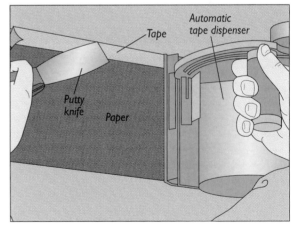

Protecting light fixtures
If you can't remove a light fixture, loosen the ceiling plate and tie a plastic garbage bag around the fixture to protect it from paint drips (right).

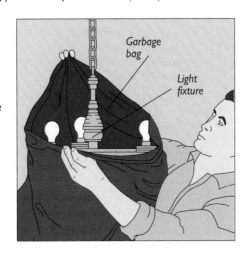

Using an automatic tape dispenser
Depending on the size of the job you're undertaking, consider using an automatic tape dispenser. It quickly applies tape as well as a layer of paper for an extra zone of protection. Press the tape to the surface with a putty knife (above) or a finger to prevent paint seepage.

Cleaning Up

As soon as you're finished any painting project, clean your tools. Don't delay—dry paint can make a later cleanup extremely difficult.

Tools used with latex paint wash up easily with soap and water. Be sure to remove excess paint before washing instead of letting it go down the drain.

Use paint thinner to clean tools used with alkyd paint. Protect your hands with rubber gloves. Since you can't pour thinner down the drain or dispose of it easily, it's best to save the thinner and reuse it. Keep the thinner in an old paint can or other container that won't be dissolved by the chemicals in the thinner. When the thinner becomes very cloudy, let the paint settle to the bottom and then pour the thinner into another can. Dispose of the hard sediment.

It's not necessary to clean brushes and rollers if you plan to return to your project shortly. Brushes will keep for a few days if you soak them in the appropriate solvent; or, wrap them in foil or plastic and put those used with alkyd paint in the freezer and those used with latex paint in the refrigerator. Rollers or applicators will keep overnight wrapped tightly in a plastic bag.

CLEANING BRUSHES

Remove excess paint from brushes by brushing it out onto cardboard; or, put the brush between sheets of newspaper and press down while pulling out the brush.

To clean a synthetic brush used with latex paint, hold the brush under running water until the water runs clear. Wash the brush with soap and lukewarm water, forcing water into the bristles and heel. Rinse well.

To clean a natural-bristle or synthetic brush used with alkyd paint, work paint thinner into the bristles, especially at the heel. Then, use a

Spinning a brush

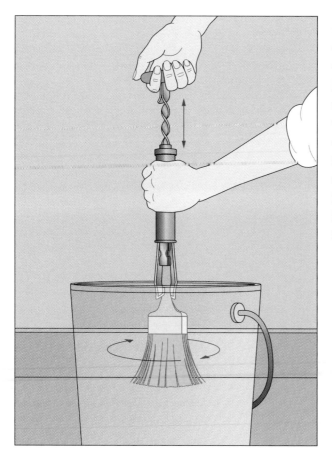

Using a brush spinner
Once your brush has been cleaned with water or thinner, you can use a brush spinner like the one shown to remove the excess liquid. Secure the washed brush to the clips at the end of the device. As you push the handle in and out of the cylinder, the brush spins quickly and the water or solvent is flung from the brush *(left)*. Spin the brush inside a bucket to avoid spraying water or solvent.

wire brush to get out more paint. Once the brush is clean, remove excess thinner by shaking the brush vigorously, lightly tapping the handle against a hard edge, or using a brush spinner (opposite page). When you've finished cleaning any brush, straighten the bristles with a bristle comb. Once the brush dries, wrap it in its original cover or in stiff paper. Store the brush flat or hang it to keep pressure off the bristles. For more on cleaning and storage, see page 59.

CLEANING ROLLERS AND APPLICATORS

Squeeze out paint by pressing the roller or applicator against the lip of the bucket or roller tray. Scrape off caked-on paint with a putty knife. Then, remove the roller cover or applicator pad.

If the cover or pad was used with latex paint, hold it under running water until the water runs clear. Wash with soap and lukewarm water, forcing water into the nap. Rinse, squeeze out excess water, and blot lightly with a clean, absorbent cloth. Let the nap or pad dry completely. Wash the frame in soap and water.

To clean a cover or pad used with alkyd paint, wash it in paint thinner, forcing thinner into the nap. After it's clean, squeeze out excess thinner. (Since covers and pads are fairly inexpensive, you may prefer to dispose of those used with alkyd paint after each use.) Wash the roller or applicator frame in thinner.

Store clean roller covers and applicator pads in plastic bags. Place roller covers on end to allow any water or paint thinner to drain and to prevent the nap from becoming flattened.

CLEANING YOURSELF

Wet or dry latex paint readily washes off skin. Latex that has dried doesn't wash off clothing, however, so be sure to launder clothes before the paint has dried completely.

A mechanic's hand cleaner will remove alkyd paint. It's easier on your skin than paint thinner and just as effective. Use hand cleaner—not thinner—on fresh alkyd paint on clothing; launder immediately.

If you use thinner to remove alkyd paint from your skin, rub it lightly on spots on your hands and arms. Dab a thinner-soaked cloth on paint on your neck and face, being careful to keep the cloth away from your eyes. Then, wash the skin with soap and water, and apply a lotion.

STORING OR DISPOSING OF PAINT

Leftover paint and thinner should be stored or disposed of safely.

Storing: Most leftover paint can be stored in a tightly closed can for several months or more. If less than a quarter of the paint remains in the can, transfer it to a smaller container so it's less likely to dry out.

Wipe the paint from the rim of the can and firmly hammer the lid on.

Store paint thinner and flammable paints (check labels) in a metal cabinet. Keep all paint products away from children and sources of flame or heat.

Disposing: If you don't want to store paint, offer it to a friend or a local theatre company for painting sets, for example. Dispose of paint only as a last resort.

Check the laws and guidelines in your community for the correct way to dispose of paint. Some communities have special days when they will accept paint and other hazardous materials for disposal.

You can dispose of small amounts of paint by brushing it onto cardboard and then throwing away the dried cardboard. A good way to get rid of latex paint is to solidify it by adding cat litter and then throwing away the solid paint.

Wipe out paint cans and trays with newspaper. Let the newspaper, as well as rags and paint cans, dry thoroughly before throwing them away. Since paint- or thinner-soaked materials can catch fire, leave them outdoors until dry.

Removing paint from window panes

1 Scoring a straight line
With a utility knife, score a line through the paint along the edge of the muntins *(left)* and window frame. You may find cutting a straight line easier if you use a ruler or straight-edge to guide the knife.

2 Removing the paint
Hold a window scraper so the end of the blade is parallel to the line scored in the paint. Gently push the blade under the paint up to the line *(right)*.

Cleaning a paintbrush

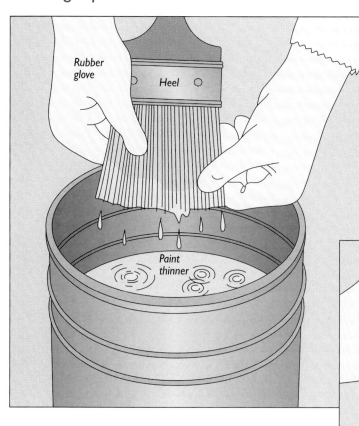

Rubber glove

Heel

Paint thinner

Rubbing in paint thinner

Use your gloved hands to work paint thinner into the bristles of a brush used with alkyd paint *(left)*. Pay particular attention to the heel of the brush where paint tends to gather.

Combing a brush

After cleaning any brush, prolong its life by running a bristle comb through its bristles to straighten them *(above)*. If you need to reuse the brush immediately, dry it with a brush spinner as shown on page 56.

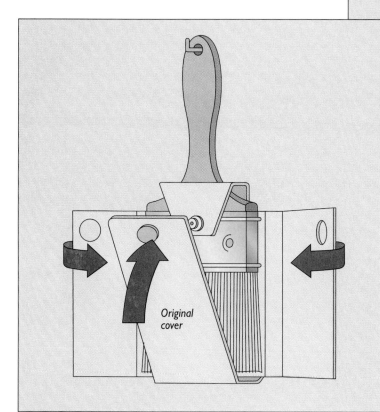

Original cover

Storing a brush

Once a brush is dry, wrap it in its original cover *(left)* or in a piece of stiff paper. Hang brushes on a wall or store them flat.

Decorative PAINTING

Interior painting can be as straightforward as producing a neat, even finish with a brush or roller. But a whole range of effects, both bold and subtle, can be achieved by diluting paint and applying it with implements as varied as sponges, rags, and feathers. Some of these decorative finishes imitate the looks of wood, marble, or stone, while others produce effects that are unique. The following chapter contains information for mixing washes and glazes, and applying your own decorative finishes using the techniques of sponging, dragging, colorwashing, marbling, wood graining, and stenciling. Some techniques, such as sponging, are relatively easy; others, like wood graining, can take years to perfect. Read the following pages and you're sure to find a technique that appeals to your taste and the amount of time you're willing to commit to the job.

A delicate blend of muted colors, sponged on in layers, softens the look of these masonry walls. The crisp white doors and trim provide an effective contrast.

Getting Started

The decorative finishes shown in this chapter are sometimes called faux, or "false," finishes, but technically the term refers to a finish that simulates something real. Some of the finishes are intended to fool you into thinking that you're looking at wood, marble, or stone. But decorative painting doesn't have to mimic a natural material—it simply can be a means to create a colorful, eye-catching finish with depth and vitality. Before undertaking your choice of technique, organize the room, prepare surfaces, and follow basic painting guidelines as you would for any interior painting project (see Chapter 2, pages 30-59). For help with color and design decisions, turn to Chapter 1 *(pages 6-29)*.

DECORATIVE PAINTING TOOLS

The tools for decorative painting vary according to the effect desired and, in some cases, include common household items such as rags and plastic wrap. Some techniques call for sponges and brushes specifically designed for decorative painting.

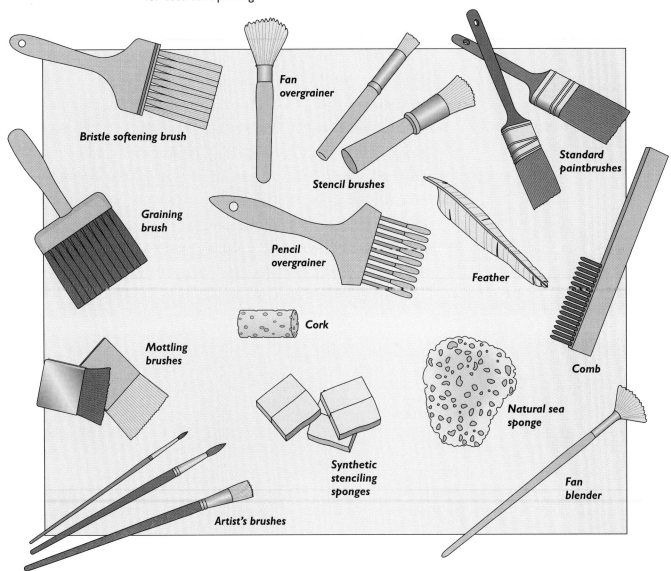

Bristle softening brush

Fan overgrainer

Stencil brushes

Standard paintbrushes

Graining brush

Pencil overgrainer

Feather

Comb

Cork

Mottling brushes

Natural sea sponge

Synthetic stenciling sponges

Fan blender

Artist's brushes

Choosing a technique: Most decorative painting techniques use tinted washes and glazes to achieve rich, glowing layers of color. A wash is watered-down latex paint, and a glaze is thinned, translucent oil-base or acrylic color. There are "applicative" and "subtractive" techniques. Applicative techniques—sponging, ragging, and colorwashing—involve applying color with the appropriate tool, gradually building up layers until you arrive at the look you want. For the subtractive techniques—dragging, marbling, and wood graining—you apply color and then remove some of it until you have the effect you want. In both these cases, the background color, or base coat, of the wall usually will be partially visible.

To give your walls added dimension and warmth, try colorwashing. To create an abstract pattern, consider sponging or ragging. If you'd like to tie together several decorative elements in a room, a floor-to-ceiling stencil copied from a design on the curtains or rug may be the answer. Marbling is an obvious choice to lend richness to your fireplace mantel and surround.

Some techniques, such as dragging, look best on a smooth surface since they make flaws more noticeable. Sponging and ragging are the techniques most appropriate for bumpy, irregular walls since they camouflage imperfections.

If you don't have much painting experience, try one of the easier techniques, such as sponging, ragging, colorwashing, or stenciling with a precut pattern. Sponging off,

ragging off, and dragging are more difficult, requiring a little practice. Marbling and wood graining are among the hardest techniques to master. Practice your designs on a test piece of cardboard, which also will allow you to see if the colors you've chosen are appealing. Be aware that if you work in small sections, particularly with fast-drying latex washes, the edges of the paint will dry quickly, creating lap marks that give the surface a "blocked" appearance. You can reduce this tendency by maintaining a wet edge as you paint, mixing some commercial glaze into the recipe (even in a wash) to lengthen the drying time, and by completing entire surfaces without interruption. Working with a partner also helps: With one of you applying the base coat while the other does the technique work, the job will proceed much more quickly.

Base coat: Examine the base coat of paint on your walls carefully before beginning. If the existing paint job is in good shape and the color is compatible with the finish you want, you probably don't need to repaint. However, if the walls seem dingy even after cleaning, if they are damaged, or if their color is incompatible with the finish you want to achieve, you will need to apply a new base coat. Doing this will save you from wasting materials and time trying to cover an unsuitable base coat with your decorative work.

The water-base mediums—latex washes and acrylic glazes—adhere best to latex base coats with an eggshell, satin, or semigloss finish. They don't stick well to a gloss fin-

ish, even if it has been deglossed. Oil glazes adhere well to an eggshell, satin, or semigloss latex or alkyd base. You can even use oil glazes over a high-gloss finish if you sand first. For applicative techniques, an eggshell base coat is recommended. For subtractive techniques, a semigloss base coat is advised.

Corners: You'll need to decide on a method to handle corners so that paint doesn't collect there (giving walls a "picture-frame" look) and so that freshly painted surfaces don't become smeared when you begin to paint the adjacent wall. If you have a steady hand, you can paint corners as shown on page 69, working carefully and finishing with a brush. An alternative approach is to decorate one wall at a time after masking adjacent surfaces. With a slow-drying glaze, mask the edges of two opposite walls and glaze the others. Let the surfaces dry overnight, then mask the edges of the completed walls and decorate the remaining ones.

Transparent coatings: A clear coating applied to a painted surface protects the finish, makes it washable, and can give it a variety of finishes. If you want to cover your project with a clear coating, use a nonyellowing, water-base one that can be applied over any finish. Choose a product that works on painted walls, not just on woodwork. Most of these coatings are classified as waterborne liquid plastics, varnishes, or urethanes and are available in satin, semigloss and gloss. Apply these products with a brush. A roller will create air bubbles on the surface.

Washes and Glazes

The decorative painting techniques featured on the following pages require washes or glazes. A wash is watered-down latex paint, and a glaze is thinned, translucent oil-base or acrylic color.

Quick-drying washes are appropriate for simpler techniques such as sponging. More complex techniques that necessitate a buildup of color, such as marbling, are best accomplished with glazes, which stay wet longer than washes and give you more time to manipulate them before they dry.

Oil glazes, the traditional medium of decorative painters, stay wet and workable longer than washes and acrylic glazes, and produce a wonderfully translucent finish. Mistakes are easy to correct—just wipe off the paint with thinner.

Remember that handling oil-base paints and paint thinner requires care because of the chemicals and fumes involved.

Acrylic glazes and latex washes are easy to use—they're mixed and cleaned up with water. Although water-base finishes don't endure as long as oil-base ones, you can always apply a clear coating to help protect the finish.

Making Washes and Glazes

Washes are simple to make—you just mix ordinary latex paint with water. It is also suggested that you add commercial acrylic glaze to extend drying time.

To make a glaze, start with a transparent commercial glaze (which is basically paint without any pigment). Then add regular paint—alkyd or acrylic, depending on the recipe. The intensity of the color will be thinned by the commercial glaze, producing translucent paint.

To the colored glaze, add the appropriate diluent (paint thinner or water). The diluent thins the paint further so it can be applied in very thin coats. To extend the drying time slightly, you can add a retarding agent to an acrylic glaze.

These recipes are just a starting point. Decorative painting isn't an exact science, so don't be afraid to experiment a little.

Latex Wash

This recipe can be varied so that the water content is higher. The higher the paint content the more durable the finish, but the more opaque it becomes. Commercial glaze is added to the recipe simply to extend the drying time.

1 part latex paint
1 part water
1 part commercial acrylic glaze

Oil Glaze

This is a good general recipe for beginners—it stays wet even if you take a long time to get the job done. Make a faster-drying, harder finish by reducing the quantity of oil glaze and using more paint thinner.

1 part commercial oil glaze
1 part alkyd paint
1 part paint thinner

Acrylic Glaze # 1

This glaze recipe is suitable for ragging, sponging, and simple marbling. To adapt the recipe for decorative techniques requiring greater translucency (such as dragging, wood graining, and sophisticated marbling), change the proportions to 5 parts commercial acrylic glaze, 1 part paint, and 1 part water.

1 part commercial acrylic glaze
2 parts acrylic paint
1 part water
2 to 4 oz. retarder per gallon (optional)

Acrylic Glaze # 2

Use this recipe if you don't have access to a commercial acrylic glaze. Look for acrylic gel medium in an art supply store.

1 part acrylic gel medium
1 part acrylic paint
2 parts water
2 to 4 oz. retarder per gallon (optional)

Faux-marble crown molding owes its realism to expert marbling. The wall panels below it are covered with a blue-gray finish designed to look like stretched silk.
Decorative painting: Tina Martinez of Furniture Art Studio

Colorwashing creates a bright, sunny finish on this wall. The decorative work is covered with a layer of glaze for protection and sheen.

Combining sponged walls and dragged borders, this regal bedroom demonstrates the striking effect of using different techniques on the same wall.

Dragging

Dragging creates a pattern of thin stripes on a surface. The technique can be used by itself or in wood graining *(page 80)*. Walls, doors, and furniture are good candidates for dragging. Just be sure the surface is smooth and regular—dragging emphasizes imperfections.

First, you apply a glaze or wash to the surface (a glaze is easier for beginners); then, you "drag" downward with a brush or other tool to reveal narrow stripes of the background color. Or, use the alternative one-step method shown at right below. The pattern can be neat and uniform or rough and irregular, depending on the dragging tool you choose to use.

Dragging with a brush is traditional; there are special dragging brushes, but a good quality ordinary paintbrush will do just as well. You also can use cheesecloth or a comb sold for decorative painting—or even a device you make yourself, such as a squeegee in which you've cut notches.

Bear in mind that the technique requires enough speed to drag a section before it dries, as well as some care to keep stripes parallel. You may want a helper—this way, one person can apply the glaze or wash while the other immediately works with the dragging tool.

Dragging techniques

1 Applying the glaze
Brush or roll on glaze or wash in narrow strips—no more than 18 inches wide—that run from ceiling to floor *(left)*.

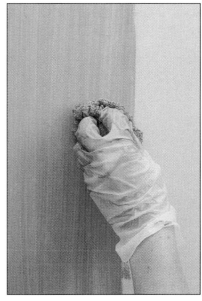

Alternative method
Instead of brushing or rolling, dip wadded cheesecloth into glaze or wash and drag downward in narrow passes *(above)*.

2 Dragging with a dry brush
Place a wide, dry paintbrush at top of strip and press hard so that the bristles bend back to heel of brush. Drag the brush down length of strip *(left)*. Wipe brush on a rag after each pass.

Sponging

A perfect introduction to decorative painting, sponging with a sea sponge creates a mottled finish on a surface. Sponging is suitable for walls, ceilings, doors, and furniture, though not intricately carved pieces. Since sponging hides flaws, the surface doesn't have to be perfectly smooth.

The most common sponging technique, "sponging on," involves applying wash or glaze (alkyd or acrylic) with the sponge as set out in the steps below. A variation on this procedure, "sponging off" is done by applying paint to the surface with a paintbrush or roller (one small section at a time) and dabbing the surface with a moistened sponge to remove some of the paint. Sponging off generally produces a more subtle effect.

The look that you achieve also depends on the colors you select. A pastel color over an off-white

Sponging on

1 Moistening the sponge
One hour before painting, moisten the sponge with water and wring it thoroughly dry. (For oil-base glaze, use solvent instead of water.) Dip sponge lightly into wash or glaze, loading only about one quarter of its surface. Squeeze slightly *(left)* so sponge is wet but not dripping.

2 Dabbing the surface
Test on a piece of cardboard, then dab the wall lightly, rotating the sponge as you lift it to vary the final pattern *(above)*. Reload the sponge before the color begins to fade.

3 Sponging corners
Tear off a small piece of sponge to use in corners. Gently dab into corner with the sponge *(left);* jamming it will make the color darker than elsewhere. (You may wish to mask the adjacent surface; see page 63.)

4 Finishing the corners

On spots in corners where sponge will not reach, use a fine artist's brush to make dots that mimic mottled impressions of sponge *(left)*.

5 Applying a second color

Let the first coat dry completely. If desired, apply a second color *(above)* following the same procedure outlined in the first four steps.

6 Sponging on additional colors

Let the previous coat dry completely before applying the next color *(left)*. To achieve extra depth, sponge on background color here and there as a last coat.

background will create a fresh, cheery effect; a dark color over a light background will create a bold, dramatic look; and variations of the same color layered over each other will provide the surface with a sense of depth. Whenever you use more than one color, the color you apply last will be the most dominant one.

The effect that you achieve also depends on the type of sponge you choose and the way in which you wield it. A large, flat sea sponge is best for this technique. If you have a round sea sponge, cut it in half to obtain a flat surface. A sponge with medium-size pores is preferred—small pores create a fussy pattern, and large pores produce a coarse

look. The imprints look most effective when the sponge is applied with uniform pressure randomly over the surface, its position changing to keep the pattern varied.

Look for sea sponges in home-decorating and art stores, in bath shops, and in the cosmetic departments of drugstores and health-food stores.

Ragging

Suitable for walls, ceilings, doors, and furniture, ragging is a perfect technique for beginners: it's relatively simple and the payoff is great. It consists of pressing a soft cotton rag onto a surface to make a textured impression.

You can "rag on"—use the rag to apply one or more colors—or "rag off"—use the rag to remove some of the wet paint you applied with a brush or roller. A latex wash or an acrylic or alkyd glaze is suitable for either ragging technique, although it's easier to rag off a glaze since it stays wet longer than a wash. A wash is ideal for ragging on.

The effect you achieve depends both on the type of rag (or other material) you choose and how you maneuver it. A soft cotton cloth works best because it absorbs the glaze or wash, is easy to manipulate, and doesn't show hard edges when pressed against the surface. Old cotton napkins and new T shirts are good choices. Avoid working with old T-shirts—the fabric has been stretched out too much to leave a good impression.

Be sure the cloths you choose are clean and lint-free, and plan to use the same material throughout the procedure. Cut the cloths into

1½- or 2-foot squares, making sure there are no frayed edges. To vary the effect, change the pressure you apply to the rag, roll the rag around on the surface, or rearrange the shape of the rag as you're working.

The effect also is influenced by the colors of paint you use. To create a dramatic effect, select bold, contrasting colors, such as red on a yellow background; for a more subtle look, use soft or pastel colors; to achieve a sense of depth, try variations of the same color. No matter how many colors you apply, always allow some of the background to show through.

Ragging on

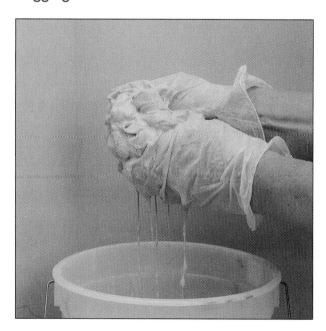

1 Moistening the rag
Soak a clean, dry, lint-free rag in wash or glaze and wring out well *(left)*.

2 Ragging the surface
Loosely bunch up the rag and lightly dab the surface. To vary the pattern, rebunch and rotate the rag as you work *(right)*.

3 Dabbing the corners
Gently dab rag as far as you can into corner *(left)*. Avoid jamming rag, or color in corner will be heavier than elsewhere. It may help to use masking tape on adjacent wall.

4 Finishing the corners
In corner areas where the rag will not easily reach, use an artist's brush to mimic the impressions made by the rag *(above)*.

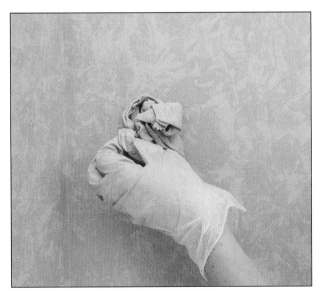

5 Applying a second color
If you intend to apply a second color, let the first coat dry completely. Apply the second color *(above)* following the same procedure outlined in the first four steps.

6 Adding other colors
Once the second coat has dried completely, apply the next color *(right)*. The final finish should be a pleasing blend of colors.

Ragging off

1 Cutting in with a brush
Begin by cutting in at corner *(left)*, brushing on wash or glaze solidly in only a small area (no more than 15 inches long).

2 Pressing rag into corner
Press a clean, dry, bunched-up rag as far into corner as possible; don't be concerned if the color in corner is a little darker *(right)*.

3 Glazing and ragging
Continue applying wash or glaze to a small area at a time (no more than 6 square feet) with paintbrush or roller, working back into previous section to blur lap lines. Blot wet surface with a dry, bunched-up rag; to vary pattern, rebunch and rotate rag occasionally. When rag becomes saturated, switch to a clean one *(left)*. It helps to have two people working together, one to brush or roll, the other to rag off.

Rags and sponges aren't the only materials you can use to make interesting patterns.

Household materials: Any number of ordinary items found around the house can be pressed into service, including waxed paper, plastic wrap, paper bags, burlap, a feather duster, or a small squeegee with notches cut in it. A feather purchased from an art store is another simple tool that you can use to make a pleasing pattern. Each object leaves its own unique imprint when it's used to apply, push around, or lift off paint. Just make sure that whatever you use is clean and lint-free.

Impressions made by several easy-to-find materials are illustrated below. For all these materials, you'll find that making an impression is easier in a glaze than in a wash, since the glaze will stay wet longer. If you're working with a nonabsorbent material, such as plastic wrap or waxed paper, you'll need to have a plentiful supply on hand since glaze will build up quickly on it.

Brush techniques: Paintbrushes also can be used to apply paint in unusual ways. Two of these brush techniques—spattering and stippling—are shown below.

Spattering consists of showering a surface with flecks of paint by hitting the handle of a loaded paintbrush against a piece of wood or other object. Stippling involves dabbing a brush in a wet glazed surface to create a mass of dots. Since this finish is subtle, bold colors are best. Specially-made stippling brushes are available, but expensive. You can substitute a stiff-bristled paintbrush, a stainer's brush, or even a toothbrush.

Waxed paper

Plastic wrap

Paper bag

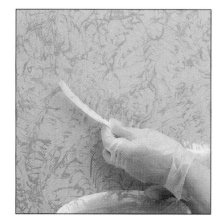

Feather

Spattering

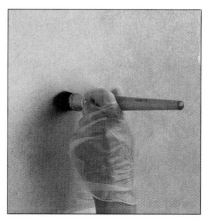

Stippling

Colorwashing

Colorwashing involves applying a succession of very thin layers of translucent color to produce a finish characterized by its rich, warm glow. One of the simplest decorative techniques for painting walls, colorwashing lends itself to a country look and other informal types of decor. It is suitable for walls, ceilings, and furniture. It also makes an extremely attractive background when you're stenciling. Since the technique emphasizes any imperfections on the surface, it's a particularly good choice when you're seeking to create a rustic appearance on rough, flawed walls.

The instructions below demonstrate one colorwashing technique using glaze and three colorwashing

Colorwashing with glaze

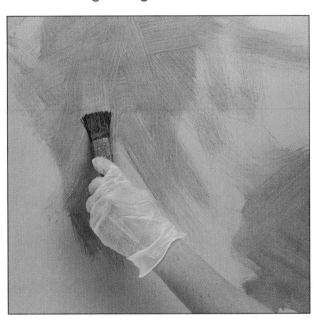

1 Brushing on glaze
Brush on thin layer of glaze (made of 70 to 90 percent solvent) in small, irregular patches (*left*). For best results, vary size and shape of patches.

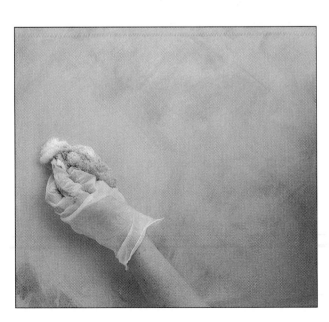

2 Blending with a rag
While glaze is wet, blend out with a clean, dry cotton rag or cheesecloth (*above*); alternatively, use a large, dry paintbrush. Wipe off glaze until you achieve the desired effect.

3 Applying additional coats
Once surface is thoroughly dry, brush on and blend out a second thin layer of glaze following the same procedure (*left*). Apply as many coats as desired.

methods with latex washes or undiluted latex paint.

Glazes produce a richer, more dramatic finish than latex washes or undiluted latex paint; they're also easier to work with because they stay wet longer.

Generally, the thinner the coat you apply, the richer the result will be. You can use variations of the same color or different but related colors. A lighter-colored glaze applied over a darker one will produce a chalky, antique effect. A darker glaze over a lighter one will create a wonderfully translucent quality. The effect you achieve also will depend to a large extent on the application tool—brush, rag, cheesecloth, or sponge—and how you manipulate it.

Colorwashing with washes or undiluted latex paint

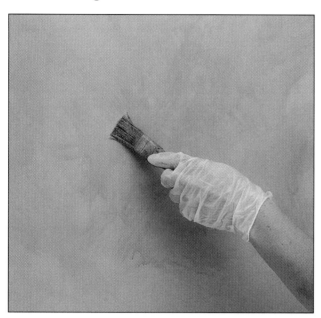

Method 1
Brush on three or four successive layers of very thin washes (9 parts water to 1 part paint), allowing each wash to dry thoroughly before applying the next one. Don't paint carefully, but rather slap on each wash quickly and haphazardly *(left)*.

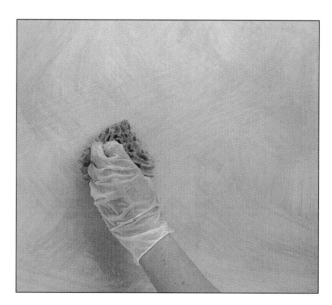

Method 2
Brush on a thin wash (4 parts water to 1 part paint) in small irregular patches, covering no more than 6 square feet at a time. Blur wet brush marks with a clean, damp sponge or paintbrush *(above)*.

Method 3
On a background of same color value as paint to be applied, use a natural sea sponge to smear on and push around undiluted latex paint in irregular patches *(left)*.

Marbling: Glaze

Marbling uses a glaze or a wash to simulate the delicate, veined look of marble. With this technique, you can replicate real marble or create your own design. You may not want to marble all the walls in a room—the job can be overwhelming and very difficult to accomplish. But a well situated marbled panel in the middle of one wall may be just the right touch. Dividing the space into rectangles and completing each one in turn makes the work easier.

Marbling also is suitable for fireplace surrounds, moldings, doors, and furniture. However, marbling ornately carved woodwork is a particularly difficult project if you have no marbling experience.

Marbling with glaze, the traditional method, requires a lot of practice and a good sense of timing—the surface can't be too wet or too dry when you work it. (For instructions on how to marble with latex washes, see page 78.)

The technique consists of applying a tinted glaze over a nonporous background, building fields of color and creating a network of veins over the surface. You then soften and blur the design before applying the final veins. (Plan to complete an entire small area before starting on a new one.) Finally, once the surface is thoroughly dry, it is covered with a transparent coating to give it a uniform sheen and to protect the finished design.

Marbling with glaze

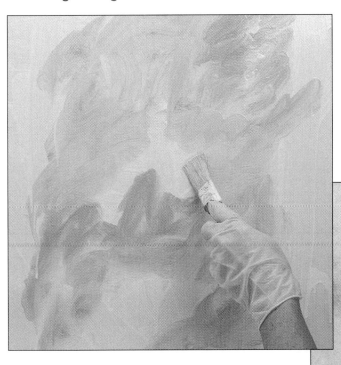

1 Brushing on the background
On a small area (no more than 6 square feet), brush on a background glaze to match color of surface you're marbling (left).

2 Ragging the surface
Using additional glazes in other colors, paint irregular shapes, or drifts, over wet surface. After applying each glaze, rag it off—blot it with a dry, bunched-up rag, rebunching and rotating the rag as you work to vary the pattern (right). Expect some bleeding of colors.

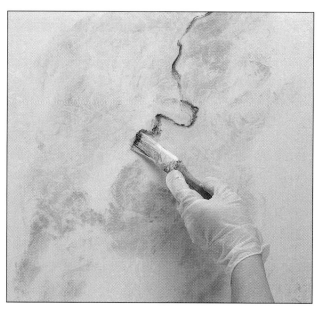

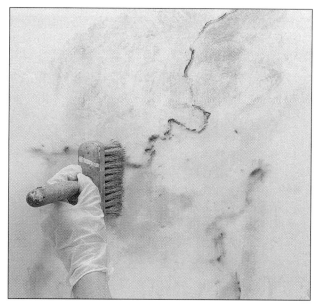

3 Painting lines

Put a dab of paint (artist's oils for oil glaze, artist's acrylics for acrylic glaze) on one side of brush tip. Holding the side of the brush without paint against surface, paint lines, or veins, with a light, shaky motion *(above)* (paint from other side of brush will come through). Blot veins with a dry rag.

4 Softening lines

Wait several seconds for glaze to dry slightly, then soften and blur lines with a blending brush held at a right angle to the surface *(above)* (you also can use crumpled tissue paper). If you blend when glaze is too wet, you'll smear or streak it.

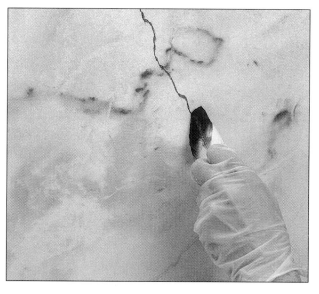

5 Scraping to create lines

Make additional veins by scraping away glaze with the edge of a cork, using a shaky, squiggly motion *(above)*. Blot veins with a dry rag or crumpled tissue paper, or soften them with a blending brush.

6 Applying fine lines

Apply a small amount of thinned paint (use a color that will stand out from the others) to a fine liner brush or to the tip of a feather. While supporting your elbow with your free hand, make final veins with a light, shaky touch *(above)*.

Marbling: Latex

Marbling with a latex wash requires a little less precision than working with a glaze, but offers just as wide a range of decorative options. Marbling entire walls and other large surfaces is much easier to accomplish with a latex wash than it is with a glaze. Marbling with latex washes also is an appropriate decorative technique for moldings, fireplace surrounds, doors, and furniture as well.

Working on a surface that has a solid-color background (existing paint is fine provided the surface is smooth and in good condition), you build up subtle layers of color and veining. Each layer that you apply blurs and softens the previous layers. The result is a finished surface with an unexpected appearance of depth and dimension.

The advantage of working with latex washes is that the procedure does not require the same sense of timing needed for marbling with glaze, since each layer of wash dries very quickly.

When you're finished applying the washes and making the veins, cover the surface with a transparent coating to protect it and give it a sheen. With this technique, you can copy a specific type of marble, if you wish, or create your own impressions of marble.

Marbling with latex washes

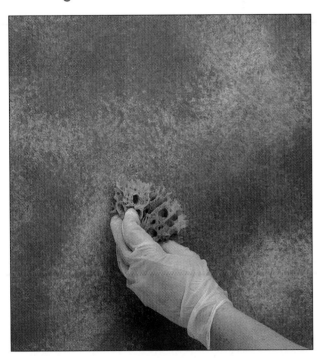

1 Applying the background wash
Use a natural sea sponge to dab on latex wash in irregular shapes, or drifts. As wash is applied, blot wet surface with a clean, damp sponge to spread drifts and soften them. Cover the surface in sections *(left)*.

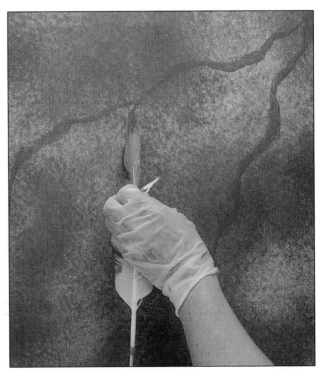

2 Painting lines
With a light, shaky touch, paint lines, or veins, over the entire surface using a feather dipped into thinned latex paint or artist's acrylics *(right)*. Use same color as background to create appearance of fissures.

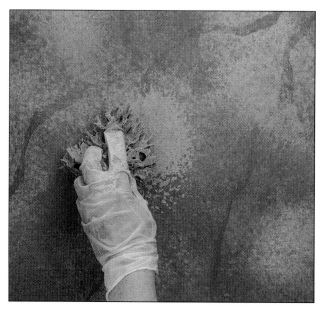

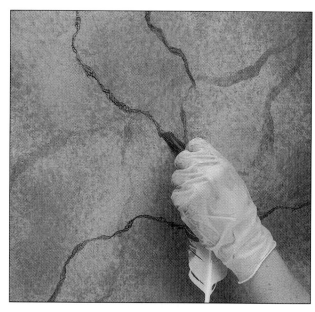

3 Applying the second wash
Using another color, sponge on a second wash in drifts, blotting each drift before it dries *(above)*. Cover some areas not coated by the first wash and sponge over the first wash in other areas.

4 Adding lines
Make additional veins in another harmonizing color using the same feather technique with thinned latex paint or artist's acrylics described in Step 2 *(above)*.

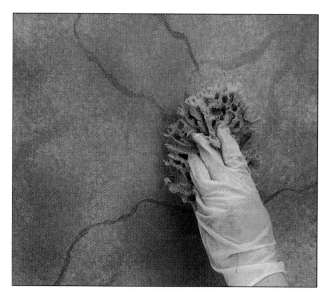

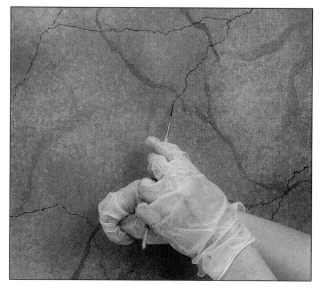

5 Applying a third color
Sponge on a third wash in drifts, blotting as you go *(above)*. (Using same color as background wash for third wash will give an increased sense of depth.) Cover some areas not touched when you did first and second washes, and sponge over portions of previous washes.

6 Making fine lines
Using a color that will stand out from the others, make final veins over entire surface with a fine liner brush or tip of a feather *(above)*; use a light, shaky touch, supporting your working hand with your free hand.

Fantasy Wood Finishes

With a wood-finish technique, you can imitate the warmth of real wood grain or come up with a new, creative pattern from your imagination. This is among the most difficult finish techniques to do well. Still, it doesn't require as much practice or expertise as authentic wood graining, and can lend almost the same appeal. Fantasy wood graining is suitable for wall panels, doors, moldings, cabinets, and furniture.

Applying a dark brown glaze over a background color of canary yellow will give the wood finish a very realistic look; you can also use reds, blues, or any other colors that strike your fancy.

Simple wood graining

Alternative method
After applying glaze, flog wet surface by patting it with flat of a brush, using a quick, bouncing motion and always working away from yourself *(left)*. This step may produce suitable graining, or you can proceed to Step 2.

1 Dragging the surface
After applying glaze to a panel or other small area (no more than 6 square feet if you're a beginner), drag the wet surface with an ordinary paintbrush or cheesecloth *(above)*. (For instructions on dragging, see page 67.) This step may produce suitable graining, or you can proceed to Step 2.

2 Creating wood graining
On either a dragged or flogged surface, create wood grain using a pencil overgrainer *(right)*, an artist's brush, a fan overgrainer, or a homemade tool, such as a squeegee with cut notches. Experiment with various effects on a trial surface before working.

Varying values of similar colors work well together; apply the darker shade over the lighter one. To create the graining pattern, use a pencil overgrainer or other instrument, such as a cork.

Once the finish is dry, apply a transparent coating to protect it and provide luster. Below are instructions for two types of wood graining. The first is achieved by dragging the surface with a paintbrush or with cheesecloth, the second by flogging the surface with a brush. A variety of brushes or other tools can be used to get the effect you want. For a mottled grain, swirl the glaze with a mottling brush.

Mottled grain

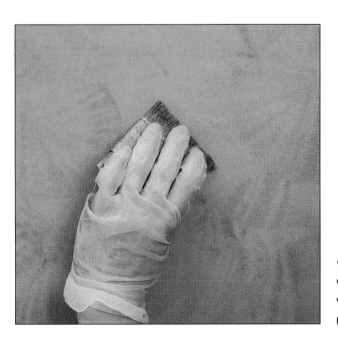

1 Applying glaze
With a paintbrush, apply glaze to panel or other small area using a scumbling, or sideways scratching, motion *(left)*. (If you're a beginner, cover no more than 6 square feet at a time.)

2 Positioning the mottling brush
Holding a mottling brush in the palm of your hand, press your fingertips into the bristles *(above)*.

3 Brushing the surface
Holding the brush in the same manner, push wet glaze around in curves or other swirling shapes *(left)*. For best results, keep pattern irregular.

Authentic Wood Graining

Creating truly realistic wood graining is no simple task. Perfecting the technique can take professionals years of practice. But even if your wood-grain finish doesn't fool a botanist, it can still be pleasing. Mahogany graining is suitable for wall panels, doors, moldings, cabinets, and furniture.

Wood grainers have traditionally chosen expensive, exotic woods to copy. Mahogany has two main types of grain: arched heartwood and straight graining. You can simulate both with a brush called a fan overgrainer. For a special treatment, create a central panel framed by rails (horizontal pieces) and stiles (vertical pieces). The finished surface will be neater if you mask off one area from the other (as shown below) when painting the design.

Ask the paint store to mix a color that duplicates the rich, warm hue of mahogany. Or do it yourself, mixing equal parts of burnt sienna, alizarin crimson, and raw umber, using artist's oils in an oil glaze or artist's acrylics in an acrylic glaze. Some professionals paint over a dirty pink base coat; others like a reddish yellow background. Finish with a glossy clear coating.

Mahogany graining

1 Flogging the surface
After brushing glaze on a panel or other surface, flog the wet surface by patting with flat of a brush, using a quick bouncing motion and always working away from yourself *(left)*.

2 Creating arched graining
To simulate mahogany heartwood graining, make a series of arches using a fan overgrainer. Dip brush into paint and dab off excess, then spread the bristles with your fingertips. Hold brush nearly parallel to surface and at a right angle to arches you're creating *(right)*.

3 Softening the graining
Soften grains by brushing them lightly with a softening brush held at a right angle to surface *(above)*.

4 Creating straight graining
With fan overgrainer, make a straight grain at a slight angle on one side of arches *(above)*. Repeat on other side.

5 Graining the rails
If your design calls for rails, brush glaze above and below completed panel, then flog at a slight angle away from panel. Use fan overgrainer to make horizontal arches—those on upper rail should go in direction opposite to those on lower rail. Then, brush rails lightly with a softening brush *(above)*.

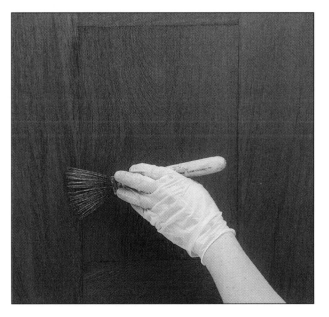

6 Graining the stiles
Brush glaze on side pieces, or stiles, up to panel, then flog stiles at a slight angle away from panel. Use fan overgrainer to make straight grains at a slight angle away from panel *(above)*. Brush lightly with a softening brush.

Stenciling

Stenciling allows you to give your decor a personal, handcrafted look that's not only colorful and unique, but inexpensive and satisfying to create as well. Stenciling doesn't have to be limited to borders at the tops of walls. You can use it on a door, over an entire wall or ceiling, on a fireplace surround, or around a window frame.

A stencil most often is repeated, but a single stenciled design on a cabinet door or wall panel can be just the right decorative touch. You can choose to work with a precut stencil or you can make your own (see page 86). Your design can be limited to a single color or call for two or more colors. It's best to stencil over a flat, eggshell, or satin finish—the paint that you use for stenciling won't adhere well to a glossier surface.

You can use ordinary latex paint for stenciling or you can choose from among several types of artist's paints. The easiest of these to use are artist's acrylics, which are water soluble and provide intense, quick-drying color. Although japan colors dry instantly, they're flat and require the use of paint thinner for mixing and cleanup. Artist's oils also are soluble in paint thinner, but they are difficult to use for stenciling since they dry very slowly and smudge easily. Regardless of the type of paint you use, mix it to a thick, pasty (not runny) consistency.

Measure the width (or height for vertical placement) of the surface to determine how many stencil repeats will fit in the space available. Arrange the designs from the center of the surface out to the edges so corners will match. You may want to reduce the space between designs so they'll be complete at the corners.

To apply the paint, use either a small-celled synthetic sponge or a short, blunt-bristled stencil brush; you may find the sponge easier to manipulate than the brush.

Using stencils

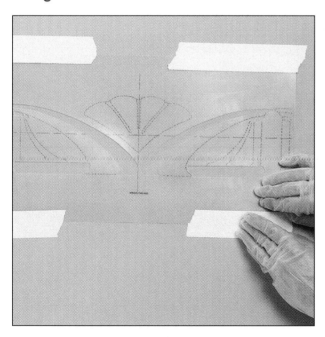

1 Taping up the stencil
Measure and mark stencil placement guidelines with a steel tape measure and a pencil or a chalk line. Secure the stencil to surface with masking tape (above). Use tape that won't mar painted surface.

2 Preparing the applicator
Dip a sponge or stencil brush into paint, then tap it on scrap paper or a paper plate to get rid of excess (above). Be careful: Too much paint on the brush or sponge allows paint to seep under the stencil.

84

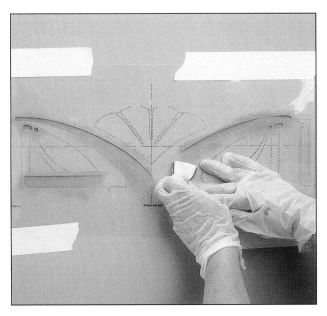

3 Applying paint to the first stencil

Apply paint to the surface with brush or sponge by pouncing—tapping it directly against the surface *(above)*—or by using a circular motion. Work from the outside of each shape toward the center.

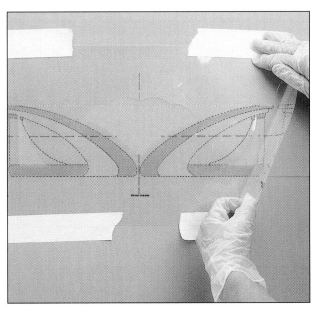

4 Removing the first stencil

After all shapes are filled in with paint, carefully remove first stencil; then tape the second stencil to surface, aligning both designs *(above)*.

5 Applying paint to additional stencils

Apply paint to the second and any subsequent stencils following the same procedure *(above)*.

6 Touching up

After completed stenciled design is dry, touch up any smudges at edges with the same paint used for background finish *(above)*.

Making Your Own Stencil

While commercial stencils are available in a wide variety of styles, you can greatly increase your design options by making your own. This is particularly useful when you want to match an existing decorative element in your home or create a motif with a favorite existing design. Copying an existing design is actually pretty easy. If the example is the wrong size, simply reduce or enlarge it on a photocopy machine (see opposite page).

The number of stencils required for a design depends on the number of colors involved and the intricacy of the design. Each color should have a separate stencil unless the sections to be painted in different colors are spaced far apart. You also need separate stencils if the design has many small pieces or lines that run close together, even if they're the same color.

Gathering supplies: The most convenient material for making stencils is clear acetate (.0075 gauge) since it's transparent and allows you to layer as many sheets as you need and still see the first design clearly. Stencil board is another possibility but, because it is opaque, it doesn't allow you to see the additional stencil layers underneath.

You'll also need colored pencils or markers, a utility or craft knife and a supply of sharp blades, a ruler, masking tape, and a good cutting surface.

To transfer the design onto the stencil material, you'll need a technical drawing pen and india ink. Note that transferring the design may not be necessary if you make use of a photocopy as a cutting guide (see opposite page).

Transferring the design: Draw the design to the desired size on graph paper. If you're copying from a stencil book, the design will already have bridges—narrow strips that link the different parts of the design and stop the stencil from falling apart. Otherwise, you must put in bridges yourself by breaking the design into logical segments and placing bridges there. Color the completed design with the appropriate colors so you'll know which shapes to cut out on each stencil. Trim the stencil material, leaving a 1-inch margin around the design. Tape the first stencil layer over the design and trace the areas that will be painted with the first color. If you're using more than one layer, leave the first one in place and tape successive stencils on top.

To make registration marks on each stencil, trace a section of the design that will not be filled in using that stencil with a dotted line. Don't cut along this line; instead, use it for reference in aligning the new stencil with your original pattern.

Also for reference, mark the top front side of each stencil and number the stencils in their order of application.

Cutting the stencils: Place the stencils one at a time on a flat, firm cutting surface. Using a utility knife or a craft knife, cut the stencil design, drawing the blade slowly toward you in a smooth, continuous movement. When you're cutting curves, turn the design rather than the knife. Trim any jagged edges that remain after the original cut is made. Don't worry if the cut edges of the stencil aren't perfect; any slight flaws won't be noticeable in the finished work.

Transferring and cutting stencils

1 Transferring the design to graph paper
Transfer the design to graph paper, being careful to include bridges between elements so stencil won't fall apart. Using pencils or markers, color design appropriately *(right)*.

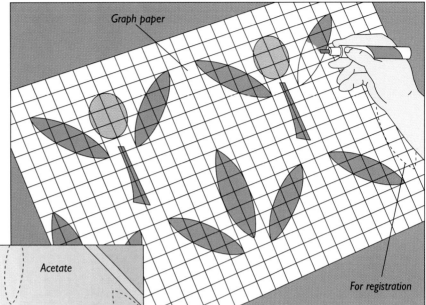

Graph paper

For registration

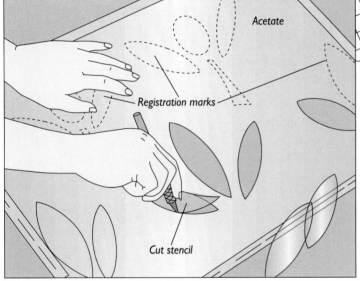

Acetate

Registration marks

Cut stencil

2 Cutting out stencil
Use a separate sheet for each color unless the elements are spaced far apart. Label the sheets and add registration marks, then cut out stencils *(left)*.

USING PHOTOCOPIES

If you have a clear photocopy of the design in the exact size you need, you don't have to draw the design onto stencil material. (Note, however, that you will have to draw in bridges if there aren't any in the design.) You can simply attach the photocopy to the stencil material and use it as a cutting guide. You'll need a separate photocopy for each color in the design; use colored pencils or markers to fill in each successive color.

To cut from a photocopied design, coat the back of each photocopy with spray adhesive and press it firmly to the stencil material. To make sure that it is securely attached, also tape the edges of the photocopies to the stencil material.

On each stencil, cut all the areas that will be painted the same color. Then cut registration marks on each sheet so the stencils will align. After each stencil is cut, remove the photocopy.

The Wonders of WALLPAPER

Available in a nearly endless array of styles, colors, textures, and patterns, wallpaper offers a world of options for any room in the home. From the old-world charm of bold floral and traditional striped patterns to the modern appeal of sleek, contemporary designs, the right wallpaper will help you meet virtually any interior decorating objective. It can feature prominently in a room, setting the style, tone, and mood of the space with intense colors and striking designs, or simply provide a subtle backdrop for furniture in a more muted setting. Specialty applications, including wallpapering borders, ceilings, and archways, provide even more decorative options. But choosing the design is just the first step in a wallpapering project. Once that hurdle is passed, you still have to prepare the walls to be covered and install the paper. The following chapter will be your wallpapering handbook— it contains the information you'll need to tackle all of these tasks successfully.

Rich, classically patterned wallpaper suits this elegantly styled sitting room perfectly. The paper's rich burgundy and gold colors are echoed in the room's furnishings, further unifying the decor.

Taking Stock

The most important step in any wallpapering project is the first one: choosing the right paper for the room. With such a vast number of choices available, this can be a tricky endeavor. Every wallpaper store has dozens of sample books with hundreds of possible colors, patterns, and textures. The best strategy is to have a clear idea of what your wallpaper should look like, where you'll hang it, and what material it should be before you start looking. You can make some of these decisions by looking through magazines and paying attention to the wallpaper in stores, offices, and and other people's homes.

Your house and furnishings play a key role in determining the wallpaper you'll choose. When you start looking around in stores, bring along samples of upholstery fabric and carpet, as well as other textures and colors that feature prominently in the room to be papered. Carry a snapshot and scale diagram of the rooms you'll be decorating to help you visualize how different wallpapers will look.

Finally, keep in mind the "look" you want to create. Style, color—including background and accent colors—scale, and pattern considerations all come into play when wallpapering a room. For a detailed discussion of design details, refer to Chapter 1, The World of Color and Design *(page 6)*.

WHERE TO WALLPAPER

The next consideration is the exact rooms, or areas of each room, that you want to cover with wallpaper. As well, consider the effect you want to achieve. Again, you have a myriad of options. Color can be achieved by papering just the ceiling or one wall. You even can have more than one paper on a wall, provided you use a border in between. In these cases, hang the darker pattern on the bottom.

Borders, in fact, are a simple way to add charm to a room. At the ceiling line, borders accentuate a crown molding or compensate for the lack of a molding of any kind. Chair-rail borders often lend a traditional feel to a room. You can combine borders with wallpaper or use them alone on painted walls.

For rooms with much artwork, choose textiles or subtly striped wall coverings. These coverings won't detract from the art.

CHOOSING YOUR MATERIALS

A wall covering's material content determines a great deal—durability, cleanability, cost, and ease of installation and removal are the most important factors. You'll find this type of information, along with the paper's pattern-repeat size, on the back of the wallpaper sample.

The use a room receives often will suggest the best material for the wallpaper. For example, scrubbable paper will stand up well to the rough treatment and thorough cleaning required in a child's bedroom or playroom. The following are some choices in wallpaper material:

Vinyls: The most popular wall coverings are made with a continuous, flexible vinyl film applied to a fabric or paper backing. They are durable, strong, and easy to maintain.

Fabric-backed vinyl—the sturdiest wallpaper—has an undersurface of fiberglass or cheesecloth. It's washable, often scrubbable, and usually strippable. It's also more moisture-resistant and less likely to tear if a wall cracks. It usually comes unpasted because it's often too heavy to roll well if prepasted.

Fiberglass-backed wallpapers are often smooth, whereas those made with cheesecloth backing may be thicker and have some texture—this tends to hide any wall surface irregularities or imperfections.

Paper-backed vinyl has a vinyl top layer with paper rather than fabric backing. This makes the wall covering lighter, so paper-backed vinyl comes prepasted, and is often peelable and washable. As well, this type is available in either strippable or nonstrippable forms. These terms simply indicate whether the paper can be removed from the wall by hand without tearing or leaving any paper residue. (See page 94 for more wallpapering terms.)

Expanded vinyl, a type of paper-backed vinyl, produces a three-dimensional effect. Especially well suited to walls that aren't perfectly smooth, it mimics the look of surfaces such as rough plaster, granite, textured paint, or grass cloth.

Vinyl-coated paper, made of paper coated with a thin layer of vinyl, looks like paper and not vinyl so it lends an air of sophistication to light-use areas. Even those vinyl-coated papers that are washable can stain and tear more easily than other papers with vinyl content.

Textiles: Textile wall coverings come in many colors and textures, from very casual to elegantly formal. They're usually made of cotton, linen, or other natural plant

Floral wallpaper lends a splash of color to this sunny study and reading room. Bold patterns such as this one work best when used beside more muted elements like the wooden desk, bookshelf and flooring.
Design: Robert H. Waterman/Waterman & Sun

The stonelike appearance of this wallpaper provides a suitable backdrop for the stone motif of the room's installations and countertop statue. Design: Nancy Emerson & Allan Davis

fibers, or polyester, often bonded to a paper-type backing. Grass cloth is a traditional favorite among textile wall coverings; its threads can be arranged vertically, horizontally, or in a woven pattern.

Hemp, another type of textile wall covering, is similar to grass cloth but has thinner fibers. Wall coverings made of yarn and string have been surpassing grass cloth in popularity because they're often easier to install.

Burlap, often bonded to backing, offers a rugged look. At the other end of the spectrum is the sophisticated appearance of moiré silks and wall coverings featuring a flame stitch or a pattern printed over dyed textile.

Hand-screened paper: This vividly colorful paper is more expensive than most machine-printed wall-

papers since each color is applied with a separate handmade and hand-placed silk screen. Some of the new machine-printed papers have the look of hand-screened ones, but at less cost.

It's best to hire a professional to hang this type of paper: Patterns may match less accurately, and edges often need to be trimmed and double-cut at seams. As well, since water-soluble dyes are often used, great care must be taken to ensure that the printed side is kept free of paste and water.

Solid paper: Whether inexpensive or very costly, paper wall coverings with no vinyl content tear easily.

Foils: Because of their reflective quality, foils and other metallics brighten up small, dark spaces. Getting a professional to hang this type of paper is advised since foils

wrinkle easily and require an absolutely smooth wall surface as well as special installation techniques.

Flocked paper: The texture of a flocked paper resembles damask or cut velvet. Because they're hard to work with, flocks are almost always hung professionally.

Murals: Murals are equally suited to informal settings—a nature scene in a den—and more elegant ones—a traditional European scene in a dining room. For less drama, try single-panel murals in the middle of a large wall—with paper that matches the mural's background on either side. Regardless of design, a mural opens up a room.

Mural panels must be hung in a specific order and at a certain height—if a scene doesn't begin at the same height as nearby furniture, it may appear to "float."

Estimating Wallpaper Needs

When you're ready to make your purchase, you'll need to know how many rolls of wallpaper to buy. Be sure to order enough the first time—rolls printed at different times may have color variations.

Measuring rooms: When estimating how many rolls you will need, it helps to calculate the area to be covered. Start by measuring the wall height from floor to ceiling, excluding baseboards and moldings. Take your measurements in feet, rounding off to the next highest half or full foot. Then, measure the width of all the walls to get the perimeter of the room. Find the walls' total square footage by multiplying the height by the perimeter, then subtract the square footage of areas that will not be covered—such as doors and windows. This will give you the area in square feet to be covered. Add 15 percent to this total for wastage. Take this figure with you when you shop so you and the retailer can calculate your needs.

Calculating rolls: Wallpaper rolls are sold in doubles (two rolls sold together), so always estimate up to the next even number of rolls. If you decide to estimate the number of rolls you need yourself, you can simply use the chart shown below.

To calculate your own rollage needs, find the repeat length (the distance between one design element on a pattern and the next occurrence of that element). This number is usually printed on the back of the wallpaper sample. Note whether you'll be using a straight match or a drop match, as shown on page 94. Pattern repeat is an important factor when you're considering the number of strips you'll need to place before you return to your first pattern. For example, with a half-pattern repeat (drop match), every third strip has the same starting pattern.

ROLL COUNT

The chart at right allows you to estimate the number of single rolls for walls of specific heights and widths. Find the number of rolls needed per wall, then deduct one-half roll for each standard door or window opening. Pattern-repeat length and other factors may increase your needs—ask your wallpaper dealer.

ESTIMATING WALLPAPER ROLLS

WALL WIDTH (Feet)	WALL HEIGHT (Feet)				
	8	9	10	11	12
6	3	3	3	4	5
8	3	4	4	5	6
10	4-5	5	5	6	7
12	5	5	5	7	8
14	5	5	7	7	8
16	5-7	7	8	8	9
18	7	8	8	8	10
20	8	8	9	10	11
22	8-9	9	10	11	12
24	9	9	10	12	13
26	9-10	10	12	13	14
28	10	12	13	14	16
30	10	12	13	15	16
32	12	13	14	16	18
34	13	14	15	16	18
36	14	14	16	18	20

Courtesy Paint and Decorating Retailers Association, "How to Hang Wallcoverings"

Using the following estimates, find the wallpaper's usable yield: For a single roll, the usable yield for a repeat length of 0 to 6 inches is 25 square feet. For a repeat length of 7 to 12 inches, the usable yield is 22 square feet; for a repeat length of 13 to 18 inches, the yield is 20 square feet; for 19 to 23 inches, the yield is 18 square feet. Next, divide the calculated total square footage of the room *(page 93)* by the usable yield of the wallpaper to get the number of rolls needed.

Calculate ceilings in the same way. Add a little extra when matching a ceiling to one wall—consult your dealer with any questions.

For heights above 9 feet, refer to the chart on page 93. For heights under 8 feet, consult your dealer.

Multiple papers: When hanging different papers above and below a chair rail, estimate the number of rolls required for just one paper. Measure the vertical distance each paper will occupy on the wall and divide this by the total wall height to find each paper's percentage of wall height. Then, multiply the total number of rolls by the percentages to estimate the number of rolls needed for each paper.

Borders: Borders usually come in rolls 5 yards long. Measure the width (in feet) of all areas you're covering, then divide by 3 to get the number of yards needed. If you're planning to miter corners (cut them at 45 degrees) around doors and windows, add a little extra to your estimation.

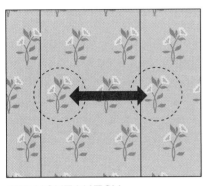

STRAIGHT MATCH

The design flows directly across strips, so design elements along the top of strips are all alike.

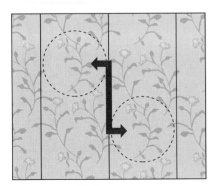

DROP MATCH

Pattern at strip's left edge is half a repeat lower than right edge. The top design is alike on alternate strips.

Bolt: Two or more continuous rolls of wallpaper in a single package.

Booking: Relaxing a pasted strip by folding pasted sides together so the ends overlap and the edges align.

Border: A decorative wallpaper strip, most commonly used to trim a wall at the ceiling line, at chair-rail height, or around doors or windows.

Butt seam: Seaming two wallpaper strips by pushing their edges together firmly.

Double-cut seam: Seaming two wallpaper strips by overlapping their edges and cutting through both strips.

Lap seam: Seaming two wallpaper strips by overlapping one edge over another.

Liner paper: Blank paper stock hung under covering; smooths wall, absorbs moisture, and provides a breathable layer between nonporous wall covering and the wall surface.

Nonporous wall covering: One which can't be penetrated by water or water-soluble adhesive. Foils and vinyls are examples.

Porous wall coverings include most textiles and papers without vinyl.

Pattern repeat: The vertical distance between one design element on a pattern and the next occurrence of that element.

Peelable wallpaper: Can be removed by peeling off the top layer; paper and adhesive residue can be removed with water.

Prepasted wallpaper: Factory-coated with water-soluble adhesive. Activate the paste by soaking the paper in water for the time recommended by the manufacturer.

Random match: A pattern or texture having no design elements that need to be matched between adjoining strips.

Selvage: The unpatterned side edges of wallpaper that protects it during shipping. Selvage must be trimmed before the paper is hung. With pretrimmed paper, selvage is removed at the factory.

Strip: A length of wallpaper cut to fit.

Strippable wallpaper: Can be removed by hand without tearing or leaving paper residue. (Some adhesive may remain.)

Preparing to Paper

Taking the time that's needed to prepare your walls to receive wallpaper—making certain they're clean and smooth—will make the project proceed more quickly and yield the best results.

You'll first need to protect your room and its contents from paste splatters and gather the proper equipment—both for preparing the walls and for wallpapering.

PROTECTING FURNISHINGS

Remove as many of the room's furnishings as you can, then cover the flooring and any remaining furniture with drop cloths. For extra floor protection, you can place towels underneath the drop cloths near the outer edges and then tape the cloths to the top of the baseboards. Never use newspapers for protection—the ink may come off on damp wall coverings or on carpeting.

You should also remove everything from the walls—including drapery rods. Before removing wall sconces or electrical faceplates,

make sure to turn off the power to the room.

Paint woodwork or adjoining walls, if needed, before you begin wallpapering; allow the paint to dry completely. You can install any new flooring—except carpeting—before wallpapering. Carpeting goes down only once you've finished working on the walls.

GATHERING EQUIPMENT

To prepare most walls, you'll need a ladder, a sander or sanding block, and 50-grit sandpaper. Cleaning the walls requires sponges, a bucket, and trisodium phosphate (TSP), ammonia, or a household bleach that will kill mildew. You'll probably also need primer-sealer.

If you're removing existing wallpaper, have on hand a 4- or 6-inch broad knife, a trash can, and towels. Also, find a steamer or a canister-style garden sprayer (available from a tool rental company), a sponge, or a short-handled mop. You might find it helpful to have liquid or gel

wallpaper remover, available at most home improvement centers. You'll also need sandpaper, a saw, or a scarifying tool.

For information on removing wallpaper, see page 98.

USING TOOLS

The following are some important wall-preparation and wallpapering techniques, along with the tools you'll use to achieve them.

Measuring: A plumb bob or a long carpenter's level is essential for vertical lines; a short level is handy for use in small spaces and to check the straightness of the paper as you work. Take measurements of the room with a steel tape measure.

Cutting: A razor knife or utility knife is used to cut paper. Get plenty of extra blades—dull ones will cause tears. Also have on hand a metal straightedge and large utility shears or scissors. Trim edges straight after hanging paper with a 4- or 6-inch broad knife—its narrower blade provides greater cutting control.

TIPS FOR NOVICES

You'll have an easier time if you follow this advice:

• For your first few wallpapering projects, try to select rooms—or areas in a room—with as few obstructions and corners as possible. A single wall or an entry hall are good projects for beginners.

• For ease in cutting and matching patterns at seams, choose wallpaper with a random or straight match—not a drop match (see opposite page).

• Choose an open, airy pattern so that the background—not the design—predominates at edges.

• Buy high-quality, machine-printed, pretrimmed paper so

you won't have to cut off selvage or deal with paper that wrinkles easily.

• Consider using prepasted paper with some vinyl content (page 91) for your first project.

• Use primer-sealer on the walls before hanging the paper. With primer-sealer, the paper will adhere more readily to the wall, but will have "slip" for ease in positioning.

• Make sure you know how to use every tool correctly, especially if it's something unfamiliar.

• Set up a large, clean, smooth pasting table and, if possible, work with a partner.

Pasting: To paste paper, you can use a short-napped paint roller with a paint tray or a pasting brush with a bucket. A whisk works well for mixing dry paste. For prepasted paper, you'll need only a water tray.

Set up a pasting table—a long table, boards on sawhorses, or a table rented from your wallpaper dealer. Some people use a stand near the table for the paste. A large plastic bag is handy for booking strips *(page 106)*.

Walls, seams, and borders may each require a different adhesive. The choice depends on the type of paper you're hanging, so check the manufacturer's recommendations or consult someone at the wallpaper store. Premixed adhesive is generally easier to work with than dry. Clay-base adhesive holds to the wall better than cellulose or wheat-base paste, but it's messier and harder to handle. Mix dry paste with distilled water—impurities in tap water can allow for mildew growth.

WALLPAPERING TOOLS

Like any other home-improvement project, wallpapering requires some specialty tools that you may need to purchase or rent and some common ones you probably already have in your toolbox. The tools shown at right—with the exception of the steamer—will be necessary for any wallpapering job.

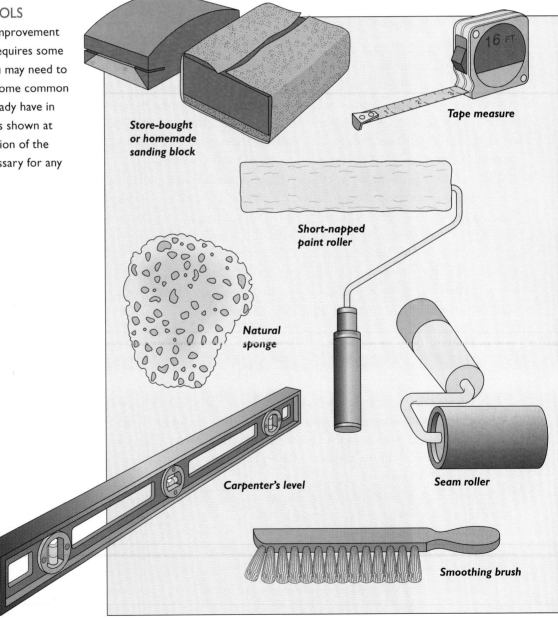

Store-bought or homemade sanding block

Tape measure

Short-napped paint roller

Natural sponge

Carpenter's level

Seam roller

Smoothing brush

If your wall covering contains vinyl, buy a tube of vinyl-to-vinyl seam adhesive. It's packaged for easy application at overlapping seams, such as those which occur at corners.

To hang borders—even prepasted borders—over vinyl paper, you may need vinyl-to-vinyl adhesive (also known as border adhesive) in tub form. Make sure the adhesive is specifically designed for use on vinyl and not on paint.

Smoothing: Work with a wallpaper smoother, a rag, a sponge, or a good-quality smoothing brush. The tool you choose should allow you to apply pressure evenly, yet feel whether the wallpaper is smooth or uneven. With textured or embossed paper, use a smoothing brush.

After paper has dried for about 15 minutes, a seam roller, used lightly, presses seams firmly to the wall. The beveled type may make seams less noticeable. Otherwise, smooth paper with a smoother or sponge.

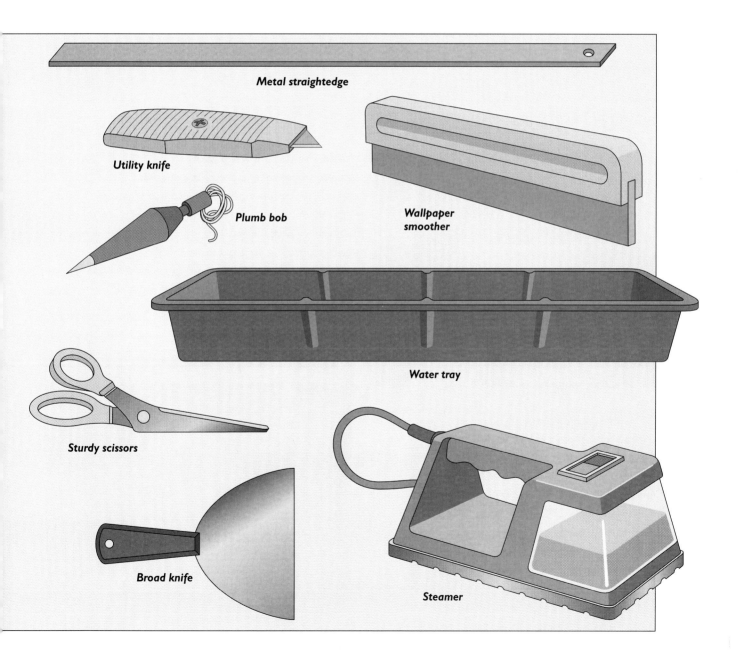

Metal straightedge

Utility knife

Plumb bob

Wallpaper smoother

Water tray

Sturdy scissors

Broad knife

Steamer

PREPARING A PAPERED WALL

It's usually best to remove the old paper before applying the new wall covering. Even when the old paper looks good, professionals recommend removing it—moisture from the pasting process can loosen old paper, spoiling the smoothness of the new paper. Steps for removing wallpaper are shown below.

Many wallpapers are strippable: Starting at a seam, gently pull off the vinyl coating and the backing. With a peelable paper, the top layer will peel off, leaving a thin residue of paper and adhesive. Remove this backing and adhesive with a wet sponge. If you're not sure of the type of paper, consult a professional.

Once paper and adhesive are removed, repair any wall damage, *(page 42)*, then wash from the bottom up with a solution of trisodium phosphate or ammonia and water. When dry, apply primer-sealer.

You can hang new wallpaper over old under some conditions: The old paper must be in good condition, smooth, and only one layer thick and the new paper must be porous. You should also leave old paper in place if trying to remove it causes damage to the wall.

In these cases, you'll need to prepare the papered surface to receive the new wall covering. If you've been using water or steam, allow the wall to dry thoroughly (about 12 hours) before proceeding.

Repaste and roll any loose seams, then spackle and sand all nicks,

Removing old wallpaper

1 Sanding the old wallpaper
If your paper has a nonpeelable, nonporous covering, such as vinyl or foil, moisture applied to the surface can't soak through to the adhesive. For this reason, you'll have to create "openings" using coarse sandpaper, working in several directions across the wall to score the surface of the paper *(left)*.

Alternatively, scrape the entire length of a saw's blade against the wallpaper surface. Or, use a scarifying tool, available through your wallpaper retailer.

2 Moistening the paper
To soak the adhesive, use a steamer—move the tool's bottom pan slowly along the wall so steam can penetrate the covering *(right)*.

You also could use a canister-style garden sprayer filled with hot water; adjust the nozzle to a fine spray when working close to surfaces not being stripped. If adding liquid enzyme to help break down the adhesive, ventilate the room well and wear gloves.

Alternatively, wet one wall at a time with hot water and a sponge or short-handled mop. Let moisture soak in, then wet the surface again, continuing until the paper can be peeled off.

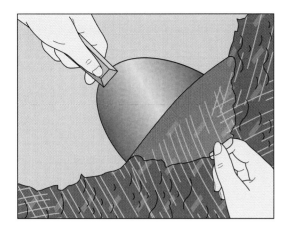

3 Removing the paper with a broad knife
Working down from the top of the wall, scrape off the wallpaper with a broad knife *(left)*; be careful not to chip or otherwise damage the surface. If the paper doesn't pull away easily, wet it again.

If there are multiple layers of wallpaper, remove one layer at a time. Sand or score any nonporous layers before wetting them.

Because old adhesive may show through new light-colored wallpaper, remove all of the remaining old adhesive with more soaking and scraping or by sanding.

Hanging liner paper

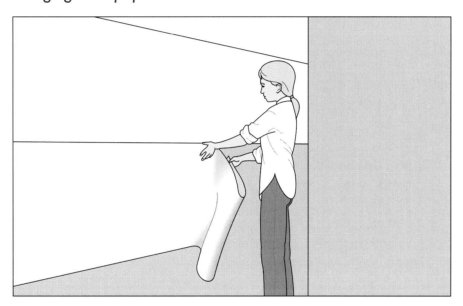

Horizontal application
Liner paper is basically blank wallpaper; there are many varieties, from canvas to prepasted. It should be used over slightly to moderately uneven surfaces and under some textiles. Consult your dealer for the best weight of paper to use and for specific installation instructions. Hang the liner paper vertically if you're sure the seams won't fall where the wallpaper seams will go; otherwise, hang it horizontally *(left)*.

rough spots, and overlapped seams. Starting at the bottom, wash the wall with a solution of trisodium phosphate or ammonia and water, then let it dry completely.

To check whether your old paper will "bleed" ink through your new wall covering, moisten a small piece of the old paper with a clean sponge. If any ink comes off on the sponge, the existing paper could discolor the new covering. To prevent this, apply a special primer-sealer formulated to seal stains.

If the existing paper is nonporous, use vinyl-to-vinyl primer. This will ensure proper drying of the adhesive and prevent mildew.

PREPARING OTHER SURFACES

Most surfaces are easier to prepare than previously papered walls. However, uneven surfaces need special attention.

Painted walls: Scrape and sand painted walls until they're smooth, then dust. To degloss surfaces, you can use sandpaper or an extra-strong solution of trisodium phosphate or ammonia and water. Repair and wash the wall as for removing wallpaper (opposite page). Once the surface is dry, apply primer-sealer—unless the paint is alkyd.
New plaster walls: Before papering, you'll have to wait until the new

plaster has thoroughly cured. This can take from one to four months; consult your contractor for the time. Wash the new plaster with vinegar to neutralize it. Then, apply two coats of primer-sealer.

New wallboard: All wallboard joints should be taped, spackled, and sanded. Then, dust with a short-napped soft brush. A damp sponge will remove the last particles of dust. Finally, apply primer-sealer.

Uneven surfaces: Walls of materials such as cinder blocks, concrete, wood paneling, textured plaster, or textured paint can be uneven enough that you'll have to smooth them before wallpapering. To check whether a wall's roughness will be a problem, apply adhesive to a piece of the new wall covering, smooth it on the wall, and look at it. If surface roughness shows through the paper, you'll have to smooth the wall. (Remove the paper scrap before it has the chance to dry.)

For light to moderate unevenness or on a small area, you can apply nonshrinking spackle or tape compound. When it's completely dry, sand and apply primer-sealer. You also can smooth the surface by hanging liner paper, as shown on page 99. With more severe unevenness, plaster the surface; do it yourself or hire a professional.

PRIMING AND SIZING

Surface preparation often means applying primer-sealer and size.

Priming: In general, wallpaper goes on more easily with primer-sealer applied to the wall. This compound keeps the wall surface from absorbing moisture from the adhesive, allowing the paper to adhere more readily. It also protects the wall from damage when the covering is later removed. Some clean walls painted with a high-quality, flat alkyd paint may not need a primer.

Choose a primer-sealer designed as a wall covering undercoat. Apply it with a roller at least 24 hours before hanging the wall covering so the wall will be thoroughly dry.

Some professionals believe that alkyd primer-sealers bond to walls better than water-soluble acrylics. Acrylic primer-sealers, however, are easier to use and clean up. Use alkyds in high-moisture areas, over alkyd paint, or if recommended by the wallpaper manufacturer.

When you're hanging a semi-transparent paper over existing wallpaper or over a colored wall, use pigmented primer-sealer. You can have the primer mixed to match the paper's background color so seam cracks will be less obvious.

Sizing: Size is a liquid coating applied to make wallpaper adhere better and go on more easily. In most cases, today's primer-sealers make sizing unnecessary.

You may consider using size if you're hanging a porous or heavy paper, if the wall is textured or alkyd-painted, if the paper isn't sticking well, or if the wall covering manufacturer suggests it.

Apply size with a roller or brush. It dries quickly, so you can begin hanging the wall covering immediately—unless the manufacturer recommends otherwise.

TREATING MILDEW

Mildew is caused primarily by a fungus living on damp, organic material. Moist areas, such as bathrooms and outer walls, are often susceptible to mildew stains. High-humidity regions also are problematic. If you see mildew, you need to remove not just the stains, but the underlying fungus itself.

To kill the fungus and remove stains, scrub the walls with liquid bleach or a solution of half bleach and half water. If you're unsure of the origin of the stains, test them by washing with a solution of detergent and water—mildew stains won't wash out.

Wear eye protection and sturdy rubber gloves, then kill mildew spores by sponging on liquid bleach. Next, apply a solution of trisodium phosphate and water, then rinse well. Let the surface dry completely—at least 24 hours. Finally, apply a coat of alkyd (oil-base) primer-sealer into which you have mixed a commercially available fungicide additive.

To keep mildew from reappearing, choose a fairly thick wallpaper. Or, use ready-mixed clay-base adhesive (if suitable for the paper) and add a fungicide to it. If possible, improve room ventilation with an exhaust fan and more effective windows.

Wallpapering

Once you've chosen paper and equipped yourself with the correct tools, the success of your wallpapering will depend on proper preparation and layout, as well as careful cutting, pasting, and hanging.

Before you begin: Read the pages that follow to familiarize yourself with the basics of wallpapering. Review the manufacturer's instructions that came with your paper and consult your dealer with questions.

Always try to work during the day—you'll match patterns better and see seams more accurately. When you're done for the day, cover wet rolls and tools with plastic and put them in the refrigerator.

Layout: The first step is to decide where to hang the first and last strips, and how to deal with obstacles. Solving potential problems ahead of time will result in less wasted paper and fewer headaches.

Since the pattern on the last strip you hang probably won't match that of the strip it meets, you may want to choose your end point first. Look for the least conspicuous place in the room; usually, it's over a door or in a corner near the entrance. Check your layout for seam placement around the room. The layout below shows several possible start and end points.

Plan another layout for border hanging *(page 124)* and two separate ones when installing two papers of different widths with a chair rail or border in between. If you plan to paper the ceiling, always do this first *(page 118)*.

PLANNING PROPER LAYOUT

Most rooms have several possible start and end points for hanging wallpaper. The illustration below shows some possibilities. You can start and end at an inconspicuous spot (pink and gold lines). Or, you can center your first strip at a focal point in the room and work in both directions (blue line).

Once a layout is chosen, determine where seams will fall by holding a wallpaper roll where the first strip will hang. Note where the edges rest. Flip the roll end-over-end to find the next seam location, continuing around the room. Keep seams at least 4 inches away from obstacles such as corners, windows, and doors. You'll want a seam near the center of each window or door so that paper will fit around it and you won't have to cut out the large openings. If seams fall in awkward spots, pick another start point. If you're starting and ending in the same spot, you can alter seam location by making the starting strip narrower. Mark layout points on the wall with a pencil before you begin papering.

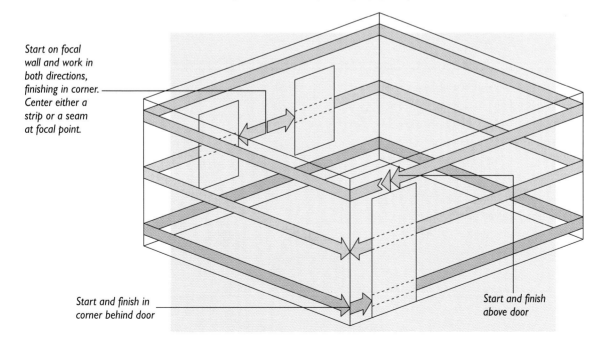

Start on focal wall and work in both directions, finishing in corner. Center either a strip or a seam at focal point.

Start and finish in corner behind door

Start and finish above door

Two methods of establishing plumb

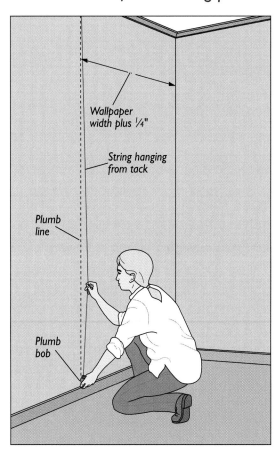

Wallpaper width plus ¼"

String hanging from tack

Plumb line

Plumb bob

Marking with a plumb bob

Begin by adding ¼ inch to the width of your wallpaper. Measure this distance from your starting point and mark the wall near the ceiling. The slight offset avoids the possibility that the chalk or pencil used to make the plumb line will bleed through the seam. Rub light-colored chalk along a plumb-bob string or another string with a weight. Place a tack in the wall at the mark you just made and tie the string's end to the tack so the point of the plumb bob or weight dangles just a fraction of an inch above the baseboard.

Once the weight stops swinging back and forth, press the lower end of the string against the wall. Pull out on the middle of the line until it's taut *(left)* and then let go. The vertical chalk mark left on the wall is the plumb line.

Marking with a carpenter's level

Hold a carpenter's level vertically on the wall, placing one edge against the mark you made (see step above). Adjust the level until the bubble that designates plumb is centered. Draw a line in light pencil along the level's edge *(right)*. Move the level down and repeat, connecting lines until you have marked a ceiling-to-floor plumb line.

Make sure you hold the level steady and that the bubble remains absolutely centered *(inset, near right)*. Even a slight variance *(inset, far right)* will cause problems.

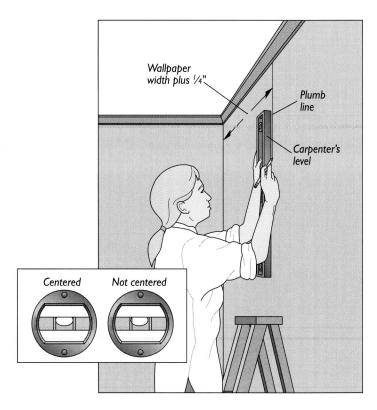

Wallpaper width plus ¼"

Plumb line

Carpenter's level

Centered   *Not centered*

Establishing plumb: Because most house walls are not plumb—that is, perfectly vertical—you'll need to establish a plumb line and use it to properly align the first strip. You'll also need to establish a new plumb line every time you turn a corner.

To draw a plumb line, you can use either a plumb bob or a carpenter's level. Both possibilities are shown on the opposite page.

Cutting the paper: For visually pleasing results, any design in the wall covering should look nice at the ceiling line. If your design includes a chair rail, you may need to compromise between the appearance of the pattern at ceiling height and at chair-rail height.

To cut a strip, measure the wall height needed. On the wallpaper roll, locate the design element you want at the top edge, measure two inches above that, and cut across the paper with a straightedge and a razor knife or utility knife. Or, make a straight crease at that point, keeping the edges aligned as you fold, and carefully cut along the crease with utility shears or scissors.

Measure the length of paper you need, add four inches, and make the bottom cut. Roll the strip bottom-to-top pattern-side in to reduce the tendency of the paper to stay rolled.

At first, cut—and hang—only one strip at a time. As you develop confidence, and if your paper has a random match or a straight match with a short repeat, you can cut several strips in a row. Always be sure to number the strips lightly in pencil

Planning pattern at the ceiling line

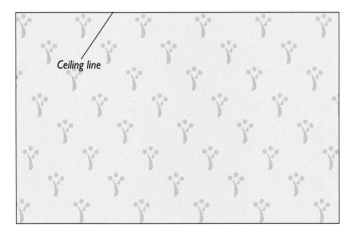

Ceiling line

Simple pattern at ceiling line

To avoid chopping the design in an awkward spot, plan to have a full design element fall just below the ceiling line (left). If you can keep a plain background area at the top edge, any variations in ceiling height won't affect the design. For wallpaper with a drop match, place two pieces on a table, match them, and use a straightedge to find the best breaking point across both of the strips.

Ceiling pattern with border

When planning to hang a border over wallpaper, take into account how much of the paper's design the border will cover. Lay the border over the wall covering on a table so the desired top design element in the wall covering starts below the border. Then, lightly mark the wall covering at the top edge of the border to indicate where to place the paper at the ceiling line (right).

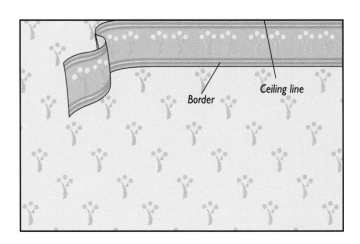

Border

Ceiling line

on the back. Cut only enough strips to reach the next obstacle, such as a window, fireplace, or corner.

When you're cutting subsequent strips for a drop match, the best way to ensure that the pattern matches is to hold the roll up to the wall. Leaving a minimum 2-inch top allowance, match the pattern to the adjoining strip and make a crease 2 inches above that match. Place the roll on the table, then make the top

cut at the crease. Measure the wall height plus 4 inches, then make the bottom cut.

Pasting and soaking paper: With some wall coverings, you'll need to apply adhesive to the backing before hanging the strips. Prepasted papers already have an adhesive backing; a soaking in water will activate the paste. Both methods usually require the papers to be booked—a special folding technique that allows the

paper to relax while it absorbs the adhesive (see page 106).

The instructions that come with your wallpaper are the best guide to choosing the proper adhesive. Premixed adhesives are convenient and easy to use. If you're using a dry adhesive, mix it with distilled water according to the manufacturer's directions until it's smooth and not too thick—the consistency should be like gravy; squish any lumps.

Pasting wall covering

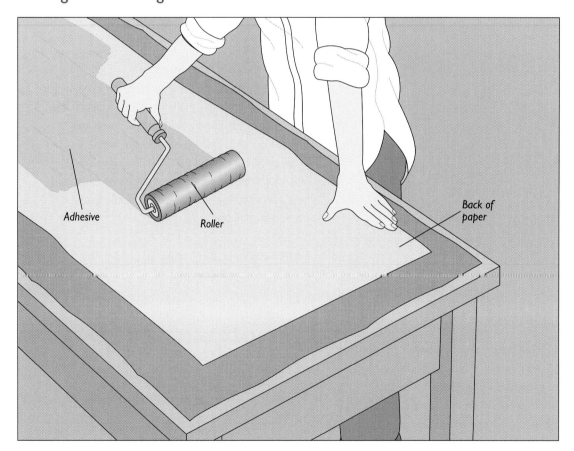

Adhesive

Roller

Back of paper

Pasting a strip
Place the strip, pattern-side down, on the pasting table. Apply the adhesive with a short-napped roller, working from the center of the strip to the edges *(above)* and making sure the edges are well pasted.

Alternatively, apply the adhesive to the strip with a pasting brush, working in a figure-eight pattern and spreading the paste until the back is uniformly and fully covered. Once the strip is pasted, proceed to the booking step *(page 106)*.

Soaking prepasted paper

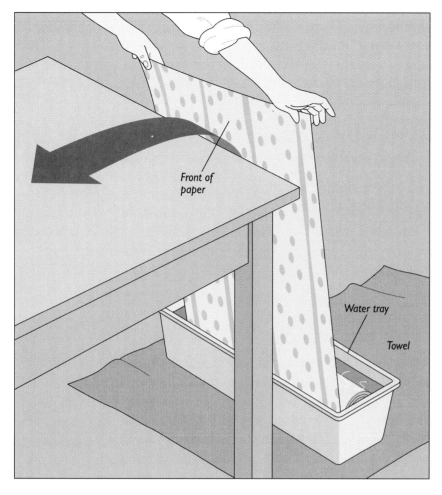

Front of paper

Water tray

Towel

Soaking a strip

Place a water tray on a towel on the floor next to your worktable. Align the tray so its long side is parallel with the side of the table. Fill the tray two-thirds full of lukewarm water.

First, loosely roll up the strip, pattern-side out, and immerse the roll in the water for 10 to 15 seconds or as recommended by the manufacturer. Then, grasping the top corners of the soaked strip, pull it up slowly, about a foot per second, letting any excess water fall back into the tray *(left)*.

Place the strip, pattern-side down, on the table. Then, book the strip *(page 106)* unless the manufacturer recommends against it. If you're not booking the paper, you can place the water tray on the floor directly beneath the wall area that the strip will eventually cover.

With unpasted paper, apply adhesive with a roller or a pasting brush, as shown on the opposite page. Cover the back of the paper completely and smoothly; aim for a thin, even coat. Be sure that the edges of the paper are well coated. Try not to get any paste on the pattern side. After hanging a strip or two, you'll get the feel of the right amount of paste to use. If the strip won't stick, you're not using enough; if paste oozes out, you're using too much. On a hot, dry day, using a bit more paste keeps the paper from drying too fast.

After pasting, book the paper as described on page 106.

Although prepasted papers technically are already pasted, some professional paperhangers repaste them before they're hung. When prepasted paper first appeared, some rolls had uneven, unreliable coatings of paste, so many professionals tended to repaste to avoid problems. Although manufacturing techniques have improved since then, some installers still recommend repasting, claiming that it increases adhesion and reduces shrinkage. Repasting also makes it easier to move the booked paper around on the wall.

On the other hand, repasting voids the manufacturer's warranty

and eliminates strippability. Of course, you could apply a prepasted activator—basically a diluted paste—on prepasted papers using a brush or roller. Some dealers warn that the added paste may occasionally react adversely with the paste already applied to the paper, leading to adhesion problems and chemical spotting. Discuss the pros and cons of repasting prepasted paper with your dealer. If you decide to repaste, proceed as for unpasted paper, but dilute the adhesive with 50 percent more water. Apply adhesive with a short-napped roller.

The technique for soaking prepasted paper is shown above.

Booking: To promote even adhesion, wallpaper needs time before it's hung to absorb the paste. Moistened paper also expands slightly; if it's hung too quickly, the paper expands on the wall, causing bubbling. To allow the strip to relax, you must use a technique known as booking. Most wallpapers, except foils and a few others, require booking.

As described below, the booking process is simple. It entails folding one third of the strip over onto itself, pasted sides together, then folding the other end over, overlapping the first fold slightly. After waiting the booking time recommended by the manufacturer—usually 5 to 15 minutes—loosely roll the strip to prepare it for hanging.

HANGING THE FIRST STRIP

The following three pages contain illustrations and detailed step-by-step instructions for hanging the first strip of wallpaper. Bear safety in mind as you proceed. Keep children and pets out of the room while you're working, particularly if you are using a ladder.

When you're done, be sure to wipe any excess paste off the surface of the strip following the manufacturer's instructions. Also, clean the sponge and wash and dry your hands before proceeding to cut the second strip.

Booking a Strip

Fold the bottom third of the strip over the middle—pasted sides together. Don't crease the paper at the fold. Edges should align neatly *(below, left)*. Next, fold over the remaining portion until it overlaps the bottom end slightly, keeping edges aligned *(below, middle)*.

With pretrimmed paper, roll the strip loosely *(below, right)* and enclose it in a large plastic bag. This creates an evenly humid environment in which the paper can relax without drying out.

If the paper needs trimming, check that edges are aligned. On one side, line up a straightedge with the trim marks. Cut through both layers with a razor or utility knife. Repeat on the other side. Roll the strip and enclose it in a bag as for pretrimmed paper. While waiting the required booking time, sponge the pasting table clean and dry your hands.

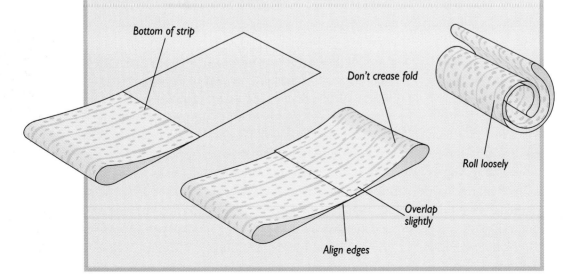

Bottom of strip

Don't crease fold

Roll loosely

Overlap slightly

Align edges

Hanging the first strip

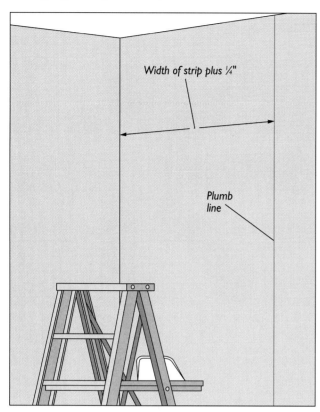

Width of strip plus ¼"

Plumb line

1 Establishing plumb

Draw a plumb line on the wall *(page 102)*, then place a stepladder next to it so you can reach the top of the wall easily. Place your tools nearby for easy access *(left)*.

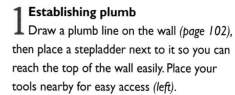

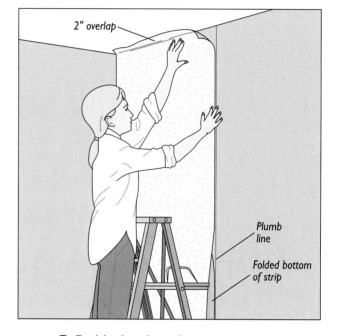

2" overlap

Plumb line

Folded bottom of strip

2 Positioning the strip

Unroll the first booked strip, but don't completely unfold it. Holding the strip by its upper corners, slowly unfold just the top portion, letting the rest of the strip drop down.

Allowing the strip to overlap the ceiling line by about 2 inches, place the top portion of the edge close to, but not on, the plumb line *(above)*. Then, press the strip to the wall at the ceiling line just hard enough for the paper to stick to the wall without falling.

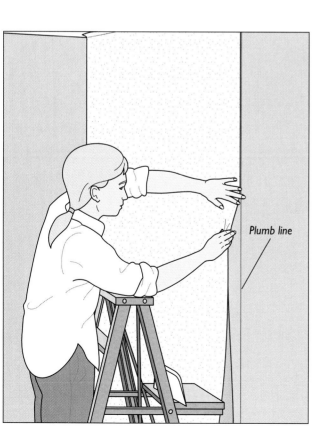

Plumb line

3 Adjusting to the plumb line

Adjust the paper until the side edge is perfectly parallel with the plumb line, picking up the strip as needed but being careful not to stretch the paper *(left)*. If necessary, adjust the top corners so the paper hangs without wrinkles.

4 Smoothing the paper

Using a wallpaper smoother and fanning out from the seam in the sequence shown *(right)*, gently smooth the top portion of the strip so the paper, adhesive, and wall make firm contact.

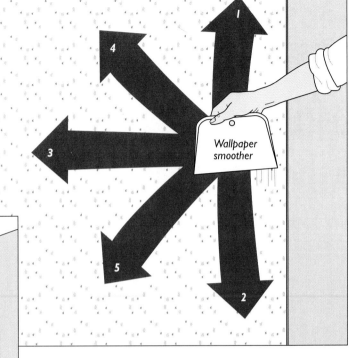

Wallpaper smoother

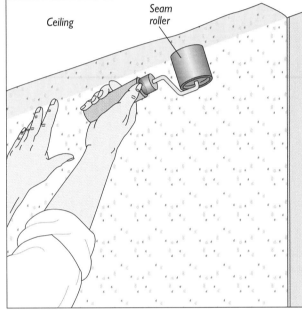

Ceiling

Seam roller

5 Smoothing at the ceiling line

Smooth the paper tightly where the wall and ceiling meet by running a wallpaper smoother or sponge along the top. If you choose to use a seam roller *(above)*, apply only gentle pressure; too firm a touch can move adhesive away from the seam.

6 Placing the rest of the strip

Unfold the rest of the strip, aligning and smoothing it as you did the top portion *(right)*. Check that the entire strip is smooth and straight.

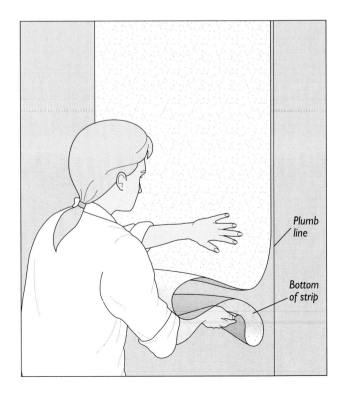

Plumb line

Bottom of strip

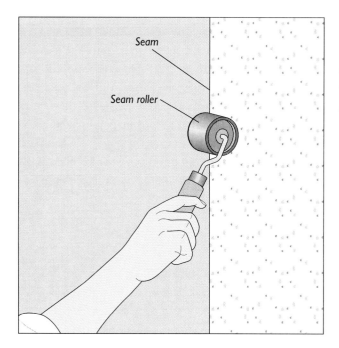

Seam

Seam roller

7 Flattening the seam

When the entire strip is straight and smooth, run a smoother, sponge, or seam roller along the edge that will not meet the next strip *(left)*. Don't flatten the other edge of the strip yet.

2" overlap

Broad knife

Razor knife

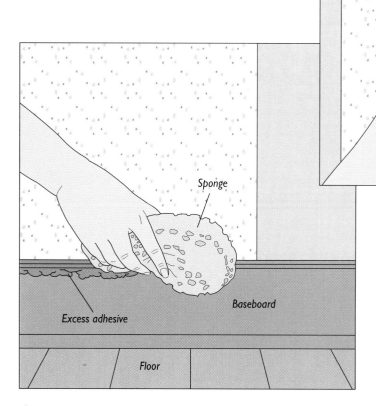

Sponge

Excess adhesive

Baseboard

Floor

8 Removing the excess

Trim the ceiling and baseboard edges using a razor or utility knife *(above)*. Keep a broad knife between the blade and the wall covering to ensure a straight cut and to protect the paper. To get smooth cuts, don't move both tools at the same time and don't pick up the knife blade. Instead, leave it in contact with the paper and move the broad knife. Change blades often, especially when hanging textiles. (Some textile manufacturers recommend trimming edges only after the material has dried.)

9 Sponging clean

Wipe excess adhesive off the wallpaper, ceiling, and baseboard with a clean, damp sponge *(above)*. Rinse the sponge often and clean it thoroughly after each strip.

HANGING THE SECOND STRIP

Hanging the second strip creates a seam where this strip meets the first one. In most situations, a butt seam *(below)* is the best way to join two wallpaper strips since it's the least noticeable. But wall coverings such as hand-screened papers and some textiles require double-cut seams *(page 111)*.

With textiles and random-match patterns, there is sometimes the need for reverse-strip hanging, which yields better-looking results when rolls are not dyed evenly from side to side. Alternate the strips as you paper around the room. If you hang the first strip with the first cut end at the ceiling, hang the second with the first cut end at the floor.

Prepare the second strip as you would the first *(page 103)* and hang it using the appropriate seam.

Butt seams: To make a butt seam, simply align the second strip with the first, being careful to match the

Making a butt seam

Butt seam

1 Aligning the second strip
Unfold the top portion of the second strip on the wall, as you did for the first one. With one hand, work from the top down to align the second strip with the first, spreading your fingers broadly to create even pressure. Move your hand firmly but gently, trying to move not just the edge but the entire strip. With the other hand, hold as much of the strip as possible off the wall so you can align the edge without stretching the wallpaper *(left)*. When the strip's top edge butts tightly to the adjoining strip, unfold the rest of the strip and finish aligning the seam. Then, smooth the strip and trim the excess along the ceiling line and the baseboard. Finally, wipe the strip clean with a damp sponge.

2 Securing the seam
After checking that the seam is lying flat, roll it using light pressure *(right)*, particularly if you're hanging a textile. Alternatively, smooth the seam with a smoother or a sponge.

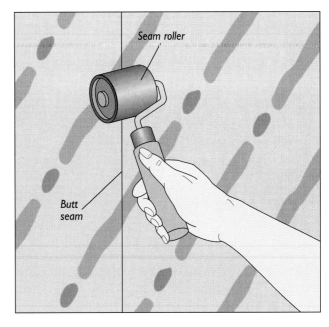

Seam roller

Butt seam

pattern—choose either a straight or drop match *(page 94)*. Position the paper with your fingers spread, but make sure you avoid stretching the paper—tears could develop after the strip dries.

Once everything is in place, you then press the seam flat using a sponge, smoother, or seam roller as you did for the first strip, as shown on page 109.

Double-cut seams: Although they are more difficult to make than butt seams, double-cut seams eliminate any gaps between strips. Double-cutting also comes in handy when you're working around wall irregularities because the edges of the paper don't necessarily have to meet flush. See below for step-by-step instructions on making and applying double-cut seams.

Applying wallpaper around corners requires special attention, particularly if walls are not plumb.

Inside corners: Simply pushing a strip of wallpaper into an inside corner and continuing the strip on the next wall can result in puckered, crooked paper. It's best to split the strip and hang some on each side of the corner. The cor-

Making a double-cut seam

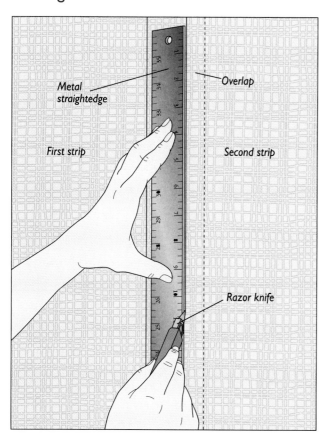

Metal straightedge

Overlap

First strip

Second strip

Razor knife

1 Setting the second strip
Unfold, tack, and align the second strip as for a butt seam *(opposite page)*, but let the second strip overlap the first slightly *(left)*. If appropriate, match the pattern. Using a utility or razor knife and a straightedge, slice through both strips within the overlap area, being careful not to cut into the wall surface.

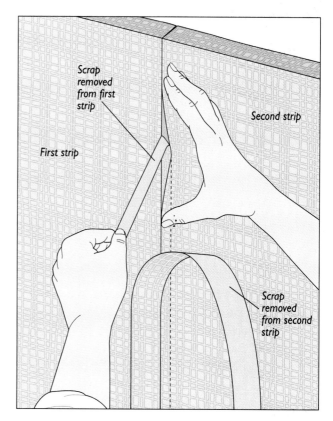

Scrap removed from first strip

First strip

Second strip

Scrap removed from second strip

2 Removing the excess
Carefully lift off the scrap from the second strip. Then, lifting the second strip just a bit, remove the scrap underneath *(right)*. Next, reposition the second strip and smooth. it. Finally, trim the top and bottom edges, and lightly roll the seam.

rect technique for covering inside corners is shown below.

Outside corners: Depending on the degree of plumbness of the corner's adjacent walls, you can use different paper-hanging techniques.

With plumb walls, hang the first corner strip, then hang the next as you would for a straight wall *(page 110)*. With walls only slightly out of plumb, slit the next strip in the middle and overlap it on itself so its uncut edge aligns with a plumb line. This technique is shown on the opposite page.

As an alternative to the procedure for outside corners just described, you can simply hang the new strip parallel to the plumb line and use a lap seam where the strips overlap.

If a strip ends at an outside corner, cut it back ⅛ to ¼ inch to prevent the paper from fraying and peeling at the corner. Tips for solving other common papering problems are given on page 113.

Covering inside corners

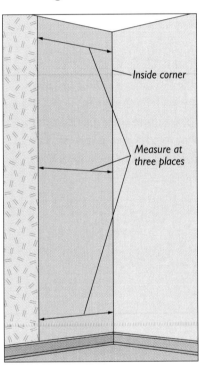

Inside corner

Measure at three places

1 Measuring the first corner strip
Measure from the preceding strip to the corner at three different heights *(left)*. Then, cut the strip vertically ¼ inch wider than the widest measurement. Don't discard the leftover paper.

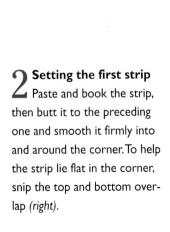

¼" *side overlap*

Snip overlaps at corner

2 Setting the first strip
Paste and book the strip, then butt it to the preceding one and smooth it firmly into and around the corner. To help the strip lie flat in the corner, snip the top and bottom overlap *(right)*.

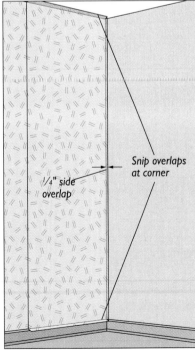

Second corner strip placed to overlap first and create a lap seam

Width of leftover strip plus ¼"

Plumb line

3 Measuring the second strip
Measure the leftover strip's width. Draw a plumb line on the adjacent wall at that distance plus ¼ inch out from the corner *(above)*. Paste and book the strip, then position the strip's uncut edge next to, not on, the plumb line; let the edge in the corner overlap the previous piece by ¼ inch. With nonporous covering, use a vinyl-to-vinyl adhesive on the overlap. Pattern misalignment at the seam usually is not noticeable.

Covering outside corners

1 Smoothing the first strip

Smooth the first strip tightly to the first wall. Draw a plumb line on the second wall at a distance equal to the width of the next strip plus ½ inch. Then, measure the distance between the plumb line and the edge of the corner strip at several heights. If the measurements are the same, the second wall is plumb—hang the next strip as for a straight wall *(page 110)*. If there are slight deviations in measurements, proceed to step 2.

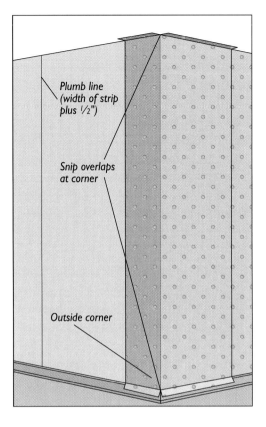

Plumb line (width of strip plus ½")

Snip overlaps at corner

Outside corner

Slit paper and overlap

Double-cut seam

Plumb line

2 Adjusting for unplumb walls

If the distance from the plumb line to the previous strip is greater at the top of the wall than at the bottom, slit the next strip partway from the bottom, working within a background area; slit from the top if the lower distance is greater. Adjust the length of the cut and overlap the edges of the slit until the strip is plumb *(left)*. Then, double-cut the overlap *(inset)*.

Solving Common Papering Problems

Some of the problems listed below can be avoided with careful pasting and hanging techniques; others need specific remedies.

Unplumb surfaces: In these cases, the pattern may not match at the seam lines or design elements at the top may look crooked compared with the ceiling edge.

Simply hang the paper along the plumb line. But with bold patterns, you may need to favor the pattern break at the ceiling over having the paper plumb. Try to make corrections in inconspicuous spots.

Separated seams: This may be caused by too much or too little adhesive when pasting, by the strip drying out after booking, or by stretching the paper as you hang it.

Apply seam adhesive just under the edges or brush more adhesive on the backing at the seam edge; press firmly. With dried adhesive, you may have to color the exposed area with a mixture of water colors and pigmented primer-sealer or fill the gap with chalk that matches the color of wallpaper.

Curled edges: This is usually due to insufficient pasting. Try the remedies described above for separated seams.

Air bubbles and paste lumps: Minor air bubbles disappear when the strip is dry; puncture others with a razor knife. Smooth out paste lumps with a broad knife.

WORKING AROUND OPENINGS

The procedures for hanging paper around openings—whether they're as large as a door or as small as an electrical receptacle—are really just variations on those for papering a solid wall *(page 101)*.

Don't attempt to custom-fit large openings by meticulous measurement and advance cutting. It will be very time-consuming and almost impossible to carry out success- fully. Instead, hang the strip as you normally would and trim it to fit lat- er. Step-by-step instructions below demonstrate the correct technique for wallpapering around doors and standard-size windows.

Recessed windows: Follow the same general procedure with this special type of window as for a reg- ular window. Once the area around the window is covered, you will have to hang side pieces. See the illustrations on the opposite page for a more detailed look.

Overly wide windows: The diffi- culty here is that usually you can't fit a carpenter's level above or below the window to keep the paper plumb. If you have a short level, hold it against the side edge of each strip and adjust the strip until it is plumb *(page 102)*.

Wallpapering around windows and doors

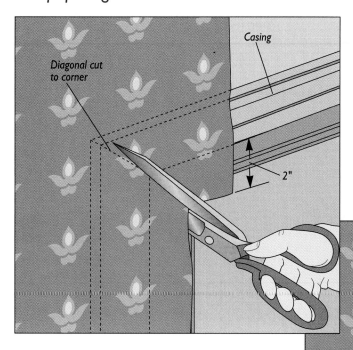

1 Fitting the paper
Hang the paper around the opening, trimming excess to within 2 inches of where you'll finally trim. Using utility shears or scissors, cut diagonal slits to the corners of the opening *(left)*.

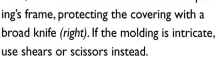

2 Smoothing and trimming
With a smoother or sponge, press the wall covering into place along all edges of the opening. Then, using a razor or utility knife, trim excess material around the open- ing's frame, protecting the covering with a broad knife *(right)*. If the molding is intricate, use shears or scissors instead.

Otherwise, using a carpenter's level, draw horizontal lines across the wall above and below the window from a specific design element in the last strip you hung. Then, match the corresponding design element in each strip to this line. See the illustrations on page 116 for a more detailed look.

Electrical openings and faceplates: For your safety, always turn off the electricity to the room before wallpapering around these obstructions. Once the power is off, you can safely unscrew the faceplate.

Hang the paper as you would normally *(page 107)*, allowing it to cover the opening. Then, make X-shaped cuts over the opening, extending them into the corners of the opening as shown on page 116. Carefully trim the excess paper around the edges.

For a nice finishing touch, cover the faceplate to match the paper surrounding it. This technique also is shown on page 116.

Wallpapering around recessed windows

1 Setting the strips
Hang the strip so it overlaps the window. At about the middle of the window, make a horizontal cut to within 1 inch of the window *(right)*.

From this point, cut the paper vertically until you can make a diagonal cut into each of the corners.

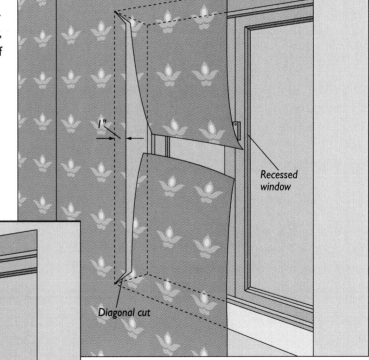

1"

Recessed window

Diagonal cut

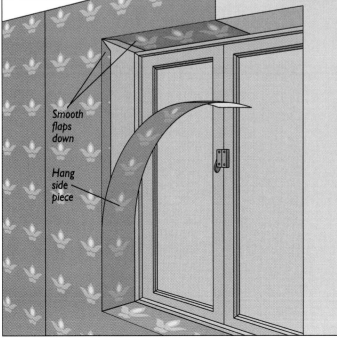

Smooth flaps down

Hang side piece

2 Applying matched side pieces
Smooth the side, top, and bottom flaps into place. Next, install a matched piece to fit the side, cutting it 1/4 inch narrower to avoid fraying. Repeat the process for the other side of the window.

Papering around overly wide windows

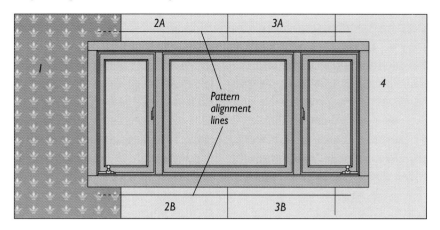

Aligning patterns

Use a level aligned with a design element in strip 1 to mark a horizontal line above and below the window *(left)*. Hang strips in pairs—2A and 2B, then 3A and 3B—aligning the pattern with the line. Hang strip 4 and make adjustments to match the pattern precisely, if necessary, then trim the excess.

Dealing with electrical openings and faceplates

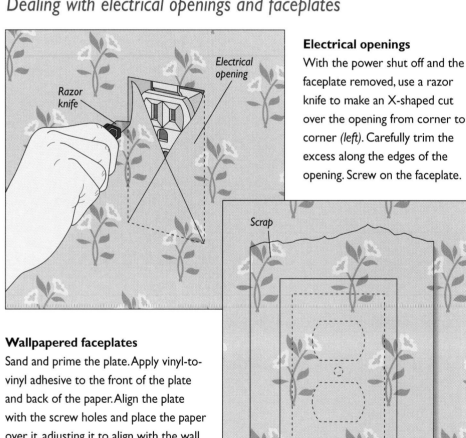

Electrical openings

With the power shut off and the faceplate removed, use a razor knife to make an X-shaped cut over the opening from corner to corner *(left)*. Carefully trim the excess along the edges of the opening. Screw on the faceplate.

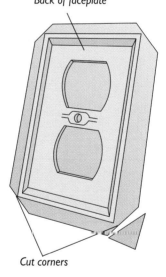

Wallpapered faceplates

Sand and prime the plate. Apply vinyl-to-vinyl adhesive to the front of the plate and back of the paper. Align the plate with the screw holes and place the paper over it, adjusting it to align with the wall pattern *(near right)*. Tack the paper and plate together, set the plate face-down on a table, then trim excess to within 1/2 inch of the edges and cut off the corners *(far right, top)*. Wrap the paper around the plate and press the edges firmly to the back *(far right, bottom)*.

Because the amount of humidity in a bathroom can vary widely—from normal moisture to literally having water splashing on the walls—decorating a bathroom with wallpaper requires extra care.

And since bathrooms are filled with obstacles in the form of sinks, toilets, tubs, fixtures, mirrors, and cabinets, the work involved can be tricky. See page 121 for more information on papering around bathroom tough spots.

The following are some general considerations that you should keep in mind before wallpapering your bathroom:

• When choosing paper patterns, err on the side of plain and simple. Small- to medium-size prints with frequent pattern repetition are your best bet. Large patterns often get interrupted by fixtures and corners.

• Wallpaper type plays a big role in bathrooms. Your best bets are prepasted vinyls—either paper- or cloth-backed. They are more convenient to use—the bathtub can even serve as a water trough in which to soak the paper. As well, vinyls are very durable and are mounted with moisture-proof adhesives. See the chart below for more details about the various bathroom wallpapers.

• Proper wall preparation is essential before papering a bathroom. Wallpaper tends to bubble, peel, and tear in overly humid bathrooms. The problem is much more pronounced in rooms with no windows or fans. You can avoid problems of this sort by taking extra care beforehand to properly treat the walls.

• Prepare your bathroom carefully for a wallpapering job. Take down everything hanging on the walls—except larger items which would be too difficult to move. Fixtures are usually best left alone—wallpapering around them is easier than removing and reinstalling them.

• If you plan to paint the ceiling or trim, or otherwise redecorate—including adding tiles—do so before wallpapering.

BATHROOM WALLPAPERS AT A GLANCE

TYPE	HANGING AND REMOVING	RECOMMENDED APPLICATIONS	TIPS
Liner paper	Easy to apply. Slight imperfections generally are not noticeable or can be covered up easily.	Promotes adhesion and should be used underneath metallic wallpapers or if walls are rough.	Apply with the same adhesive used to hang wallpaper. Available in a variety of weights and thicknesses.
Cloth-backed vinyl	Moderately easy to hang and remove. Paper is strippable.	Rooms with high humidity and heavy traffic.	Somewhat stiff; difficult to fit around obstacles.
Paper-backed vinyl	Easy to hang and remove. Paper is strippable.	Rooms with high humidity and heavy traffic.	Overlaps require sealing with vinyl-to-vinyl adhesive.
Shiny vinyl	Moderately easy to hang and remove. Paper is strippable.	Best in high humidity, windowless bathrooms.	Requires liner paper underneath.
Handprinted paper	Difficult to hang and remove. Paper usually is not strippable.	Ideal for powder room (no shower or bathtub). Use in full bathroom only when walls are treated with a stain-resistant spray finish, available at most supply stores.	Excessive water from splashing may cause colors to run. For finished look, unprinted edges must be trimmed afterwards.
Foil	Difficult to hang and remove. Paper usually is not strippable.	Ideal for high-humidity rooms.	Requires liner paper underneath. Creases easily; hang with care.

Special Wallpapering Techniques

Wallpapering around bulky, immovable objects or curved shapes requires some special techniques. Here's how to achieve good results.

Archways: Plan your layout carefully before you begin this papering job. Step-by-step instructions on the opposite page provide the information you need.

Ceilings: Extending wallpaper across the ceiling can unify a decorating scheme and add drama to a room. For best results, choose a random pattern so you won't have to worry about pattern matches at the ceiling line. Run the strips across the ceiling's shorter length—they'll be more manageable. The technique is shown on the opposite page.

Soffits: Soffits can be papered either on the front and bottom or on the front alone.

When papering the front of a soffit, simply hang the strips from the ceiling, leaving the underside untrimmed until the entire soffit is covered. Then, trim the bottom.

When papering both the front and bottom, proceed as for an outside corner *(page 113)*. Hang the paper from the soffit's ceiling line, over the front edge, and along the soffit's bottom to the wall. In this case, you should always cover the soffit before papering the wall, leaving a ¼-inch overlap along the top of the wall. Cut the wall piece to cover this overlap, then use vinyl-to-vinyl adhesive to join the seam.

If the soffit is not plumb and square, strips along its front edge will be misaligned. In this case, wallpaper the underside first, leaving overlaps along the wall and front edge. Then, hang paper along the soffit's front—use vinyl-to-vinyl adhesive to seal overlaps. Finally, finish the rest of the wall.

Wallpapering this sunny sitting room incorporates several of the special techniques described above, including those for soffits, ceilings, and archways.
Window Treatment: Rossetti & Corriea

Wallpapering archways and ceilings

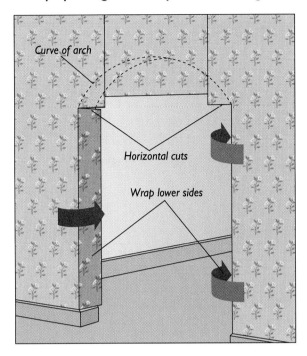

Curve of arch

Horizontal cuts

Wrap lower sides

1 Hanging archway strips

Hang the strips at the archway *(above)*—the amount of each side strip that hangs inside the arch should at least equal the depth of the archway.

Just below the curve, make a horizontal cut in each side strip from the inner edge to within 1 inch of the wall. Then, wrap and smooth the lower portion of each side strip around the arch's edge.

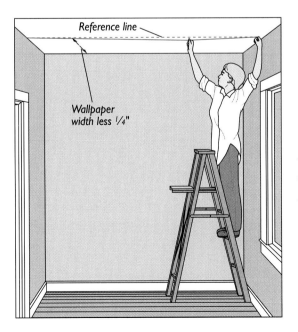

Reference line

Wallpaper width less ¼"

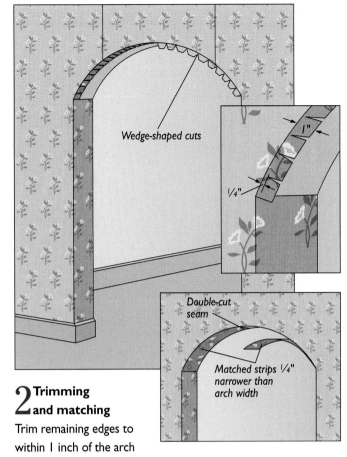

Wedge-shaped cuts

1"

¼"

Double-cut seam

Matched strips ¼" narrower than arch width

2 Trimming and matching

Trim remaining edges to within 1 inch of the arch *(above)*. Using utility shears or scissors, make small, wedge-shaped cuts along the strip's unwrapped edge to within ¼ inch of the arch's edge *(inset, top)*. Smooth down the paper—with thick stock, spackle the area between pieces to ensure a smooth surface.

Hang matched strips from each wrapped strip to the top of the arch, cutting strips ¼ inch narrower than the arch width to prevent fraying or peeling *(inset, bottom)*. Apply the strips from side to top, double-cutting the seam *(page 111)* at the top.

Wallpapering a ceiling

To establish a reference line, mark the paper's width minus ¼ inch on the ceiling, measuring out from the corners. Snap a chalk line at the marks *(left)*. Cut the paper to size, allowing an extra 2 inches at the ends and a ½ inch overlap at the side edges. Book the strips *(page 106)*.

Proceed as for walls *(page 101)*, but use a ladder and have a helper hold the remaining length while you align the paper. Begin on the focal side of the ceiling. Trim the overlaps at the ceiling line to ½ inch. Crease the wall strips at the ceiling line, then trim along the crease.

Fixtures and pipes: Wet wallpaper conducts electricity, and foil wallpaper is an especially good conductor. Before papering around thermostats, switches, or any other electrical obstructions, switch off the power to the room to avoid any risk of electric shock.

If you're papering around a large object, first disassemble the parts that you can easily remove, then follow the technique for light fixtures described below.

If you're papering around a sink or other fixture that doesn't abut the wall tightly, trim the paper, leaving a generous amount of excess, and then carefully tuck the excess behind the fixture using a smoother or broad knife.

When papering around small obstacles, apply the technique for thermostats that is described on the opposite page.

Wallpapering around light fixtures

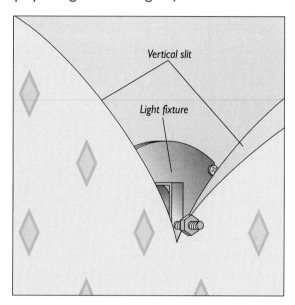

Vertical slit

Light fixture

1 Setting paper around the obstruction
Slit the wallpaper to the center of the fixture *(left)*, cutting vertically from the top or bottom—unless the side edge is much closer. Work the wallpaper all around the fixture.

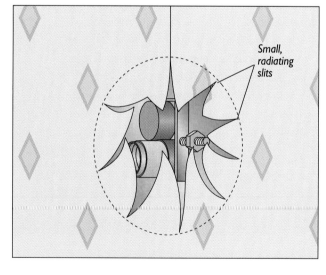

Small, radiating slits

2 Cutting slits
Cut a series of slits from the fixture's center to its outer edges *(above)* until you can smooth down the paper all around the object.

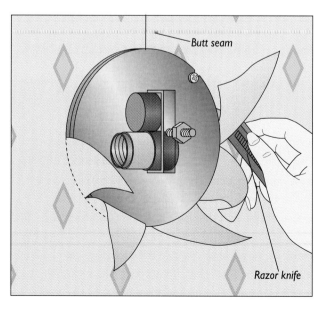

Butt seam

Razor knife

3 Finishing up
Butt the edges of the vertical slit together tightly. Trim the excess wallpaper around the fixture with a razor or utility knife *(left)*.

Wallpapering around small objects

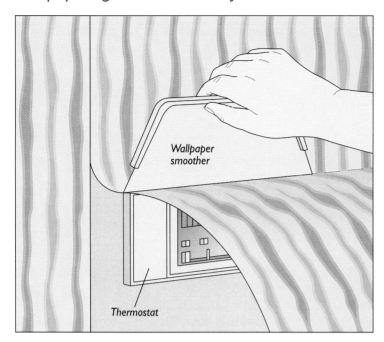

Wallpaper smoother

Thermostat

Wallpapering around a thermostat
Hang the strip from the ceiling line as you normally would *(page 101)*. When you approach the thermostat, simply smooth the paper down as close to it as you can get without covering it *(left)*. Then, make an X-shaped cut over the thermostat, enlarging the hole as needed until the paper lies flat above and below it. Smooth the paper, then trim the excess.

PAPERING AROUND BATHROOM TOUGH SPOTS

Working around objects in the bathroom can be especially tricky because they usually are either immovable or don't allow for much working space.

To wallpaper around sink brackets, towel bars, or towel hooks, smooth the strip of paper down as close to the object as possible, then cut a small X in the paper over the object and gradually enlarge the hole until the paper can be smoothed into place around the object. Finally, trim the excess.

When working around plumbing fixtures, if there is a fixture collar, slide it away from the wall. Hang the strip of paper, slitting it to fit around the fixture, then trim the paper closely around the fixture. Smooth the cut edges with your fingers, then slide the collar back into place against the wall.

Work wallpaper behind a toilet tank or a pedestal sink with one hand above and one hand below the object *(right)*. Align the pattern, then press the strip into place. Smooth difficult-to-reach areas with a small paint roller or a long, soft brush. If you can't fit these objects into the space behind the object, try a long ruler wrapped in a soft, thin towel. Gently smooth the paper until it lies flat.

STAIRWAYS

When planning to wallpaper stairway walls, be sure to purchase a little extra paper—about one roll more than you've calculated—to ensure that there's enough for trimming the angled bottoms of the strips just above the stairs on the large well wall.

It's best to go with a small, random design or a simple repeating pattern—you won't have to worry about matching along long stairway strips. Plus, slight mismatches will be less noticeable.

The steps on these pages show how to paper a stairway. Prepare the surfaces *(page 98)* and paste, soak, and book the wallpaper as usual *(page 104)*; having a helper on hand is recommended. If the ceiling is more than 8 feet above the upper floor, have a professional set up scaffolding. Work very carefully on ladders and scaffolding.

Wallpapering stairways

1 Hanging the first strip
Set up a platform: To protect the wall, fit the tops of a straight ladder's rails with rubber pads. Lean the ladder against the head wall at approximately the angle shown. Place a stepladder at the top of the stairs and run doubled planks level from one of its lower rungs to an upper rung of the straight ladder. Adjust the straight ladder, if necessary.

To ensure the well-wall strips are plumb, begin papering with the longest strip—where the well wall meets the head wall. This also will ensure you have strips that are long enough to run ceiling-to-floor. When cutting each strip, allow **4** inches for overlap at the top and bottom. Mark a plumb line from the ceiling to the floor one strip width from the corner. Hang the first strip along the plumb line, allowing it to overlap the ceiling by 2 inches. Unfold the rest of the strip, then smooth and trim the top section *(right)*. Smooth and trim the bottom section, then roll the seam and smooth the entire strip.

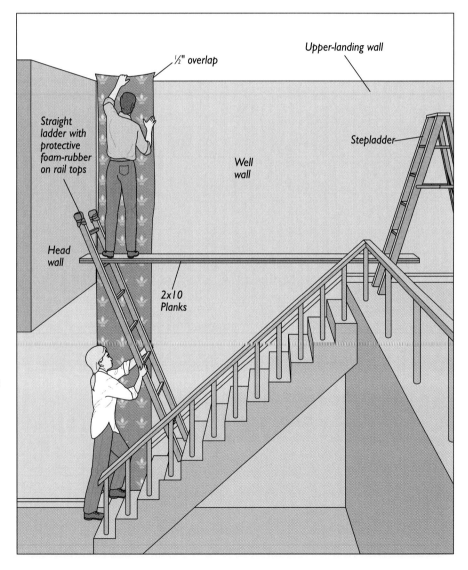

Upper-landing wall

½" overlap

Well wall

Stepladder

Straight ladder with protective foam-rubber on rail tops

Head wall

2x10 Planks

2 Finishing the well wall

Finish the rest of the well wall *(right)* using the same method as for the first strip, trimming the top flush with the ceiling line and trimming the bottom flush with the top of the baseboard. Continue papering as far as you intend to go across the upper-landing wall, removing the scaffolding if necessary.

Trim the 2" ceiling overlap

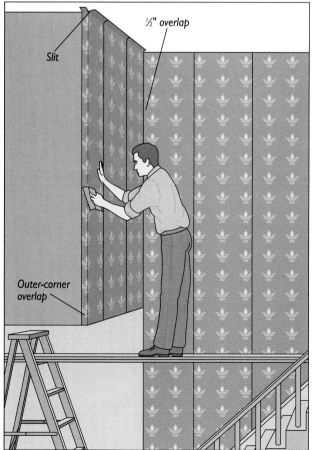

½" overlap

Slit

Outer-corner overlap

3 Finishing the head wall

With the scaffolding set up as for Step 2, mark a plumb line on the head wall for the first strip, allowing for a ½ inch overlap at the well wall. Cut this strip as long as the height of the head wall—excluding moldings, if any—plus 4 inches. Hang the top of the first strip, aligning one edge against the plumb line and overlapping the corner onto the well wall.

Hang the tops of the rest of the strips until less than a strip width remains. At this point, cut a partial strip for the outer corner—measure for a 1-inch corner overlap. Hang the top of the strip, slitting it at the top so it will fit flat around the corner. Reposition the platform as shown at left so you can reach the bottom of the head wall. Hang the bottom of the strips, slit the corner strip at the bottom corner, then smooth and trim the paper *(left)*.

The strip bottoms should be flush with the bottom of the head wall. Reposition the platform again to trim and smooth the strips at the ceiling line.

Decorating with Borders

Bordering with wallpaper adds decorative flair to any room in the home. Very popular as wall design accents—either alone or with one or even two coordinating wallpapers—borders are especially effective along the ceiling line or at chair-rail height.

When bordering over a painted wall, prepare the wall accordingly *(page 98)*. If you're using primer-sealer, coat just the area that the border will cover. Let any new wall covering dry thoroughly before placing a border over it so the border's weight won't pull it from the wall.

Bordering is just like hanging wallpaper, only easier. Be careful to draw layout lines with extra care, however, especially if you're combining borders and wallpaper. Layout is key to an attractive look.

CEILING-LINE BORDERS

When hanging a ceiling border over a painted wall or over paper with a random match, simply place the top of the border at the ceiling or molding edge. When hanging over paper with a straight or drop match, check the wall height in several places to see if it varies. If it doesn't and the paper is plumb, hang the border flush against the ceiling or molding. If wall height does vary, you'll need to mark layout lines.

Layout: To lay out a border, subtract its height from the shortest wall height. Use a carpenter's level to

A chair-rail border *(above)* stylishly links two different wallpaper patterns.

Ceiling-line borders define and outline the walls and ceiling in this Latin-inspired sitting room *(right)*. The border color is reflected in the tile floor, the bench's fabric, and the floor rug.

mark the wall all around the room at this distance from the floor.

To work around an inside corner, hold the level across the corner so one end of the level touches each wall; make a mark on the new wall, then carefully connect the lines into the corner.

Because the ceiling edge may not be perfectly horizontal, you'll need to make adjustments as you hang. Fill in occasional gaps above the border with border-edge scrap or use pigmented primer-sealer tinted the background color of the border. Or, wrap a bit of the border onto the ceiling. If an uneven ceiling line becomes a big problem, you may want to reconsider using a border.

Installation: Applying a ceiling-line border is an easy process. Simply paste the strip with the appropriate adhesive or, if the border is prepasted, soak it in water. Book the paper pasted-sides together.

Align the first part of the border with the guideline, then smooth that section to the wall. Hang an arm's length of paper at a time—any more is cumbersome.

When joining two pieces together in the middle of a wall, however, cut the pieces extra long, then overlap the ends where they meet until the pattern matches. Double-cut the ends in an inconspicuous place, then remove the waste and smooth the seam. Double-cutting around a design element will further camouflage the seam.

Illustrated instructions for hanging ceiling-line borders over existing paper are featured on page 126.

This chair-rail border, with its playing-card motif, is the perfect complement to the playful, Southwestern style of this den.

CHAIR-RAIL BORDERS

When using a border at chair-rail height, you can hang it alone, coordinate it with another wallpaper either below or above, or combine it with paper below and above. How you draw layout lines and install the border paper will depend on how many papers you're hanging. Always use a pencil, not ink, for layout lines.

Begin by deciding on the height that you want to place the border. For example, you may want the lower edge to align with the bottom of a window molding or with some other architectural feature.

Chair-rail border only: When hanging border paper alone, mark all

Hanging a ceiling border over wallpaper

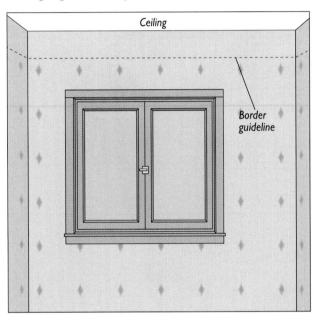

Ceiling

Border guideline

1 Drawing layout lines
If the border is going to be applied over paper with a straight or drop match and wall height varies slightly, determine the shortest wall height and subtract the border width. Then, mark a guideline at this height around the entire room *(left)* using a carpenter's level.

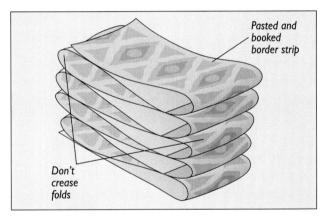

Pasted and booked border strip

Don't crease folds

2 Preparing border strips
Paste the entire strip with appropriate adhesive or soak a prepasted border. Use vinyl-to-vinyl adhesive when hanging over vinyl wallpaper. Book the border accordion-style without creasing the folds *(above)*.

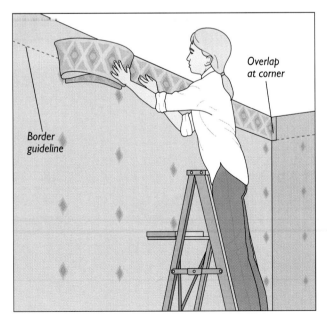

Border guideline

Overlap at corner

3 Hanging strips
Unfold and tack up an arm's length of paper at a time *(left)*. Align the paper with any guidelines you drew by pushing it around with your spread fingers. Smooth the strip and wipe off excess adhesive. If the design element at the end of the first strip matches the design at the beginning of the next, simply butt strips together *(page 110)*. Otherwise, overlap the paper to get a match and double-cut the seam *(page 112)*. At inside corners, use lap seams as for wallpaper. To precisely match patterns at corners, join strips with double-cut seams.

around the room where the top or bottom edge will lie using the same technique as for ceiling borders. Hang the paper, aligning the edge with the guideline.

With paper above or below: For this decorative choice, draw layout lines for the top and bottom edges of the border. For wallpaper below, hang the wallpaper so it just overlaps the lower line. Using the upper line as a guide, hang the border. Cut the paper just below the border, peel up the border's bottom edge, and remove the excess wallpaper.

See below for more on hanging a border with wallpaper below. For wallpaper above the border, hang it so it overlaps the upper guideline and proceed as appropriate.

With wallpaper above and below: Use a level to draw a horizontal line on the wall at about the middle of the border area. Hang the upper paper to just below the line.

Butt or double-cut the second paper where it meets the first. Then, hang the border. Keep in mind the vertical placement of the two papers so the border doesn't cut off their designs. For step-by-step instructions on hanging a border with two different wallpapers, see page 128.

Chair-rail border with wallpaper below

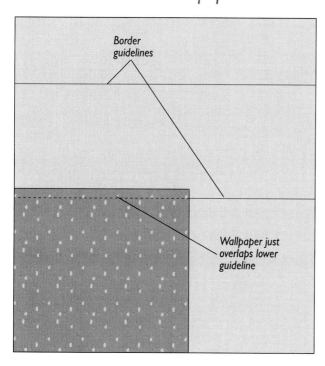

Border guidelines

Wallpaper just overlaps lower guideline

1 Setting border guidelines
Using a carpenter's level, draw border guidelines for the top and bottom edges of the border. Hang wallpaper across the first wall, allowing it to slightly overlap the lower guideline *(left)*.

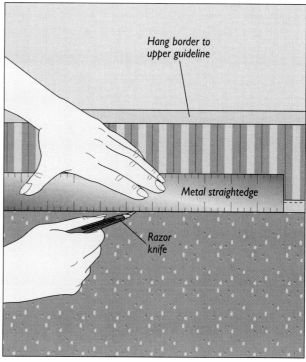

Hang border to upper guideline

Metal straightedge

Razor knife

2 Hanging the border
Using the upper line as a guide, hang the border. Hold a straightedge or broad knife at the bottom edge of the border and cut excess paper underneath it *(right)*. Lift up the lower edge of the border and remove the excess paper. Smooth down the border and roll the seam. Complete the room one wall at a time.

Chair-rail border with two wallpapers

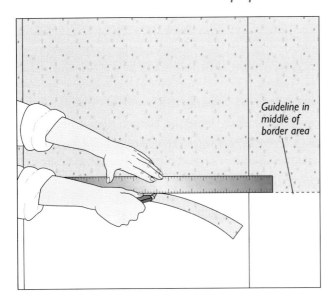

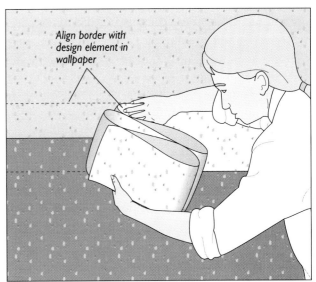

Guideline in middle of border area

Align border with design element in wallpaper

1 Drawing a guideline

Draw a line on the wall at about the middle of the border area. Hang a strip of the top paper to just below the line, then trim the paper to the line with a razor knife guided by a straightedge *(above)*. You'll be able to see the line on either side of the strip. Continue all around the room until all the top paper is hung.

2 Finishing the job

Hang the bottom strips, butting or double-cutting the ends where they meet the wallpaper above. Finally, hang the border *(above)*, aligning it with a design element on the wallpaper or with a new line drawn on the wallpaper.

BORDERING AROUND DOORS AND WINDOWS

When two border strips intersect at different angles, you can achieve pattern continuity by matching the design and making a mitered double-cut, as illustrated at right. This technique works best with nondirectional border designs since there is no worry about having to match up patterns along the vertical and horizontal casings of either a door or a window.

On the pasting table, arrange the two strips so that the pattern matches and the pieces completely overlap in the corner. With some patterns, you may want to line up a specific design element over the center of the opening. Next, install the first strip following the same procedure as for cutting, pasting, soaking, booking, and hanging other wallpaper *(page 101)*.

Hang the second strip lightly, matching the pattern again. Double-cut diagonally through both strips using either a razor or utility knife and a carpenter's triangle *(right)*. Trim and remove the scrap on top and underneath the strips. Finally, roll the seam lightly. Repeat for the other strips.

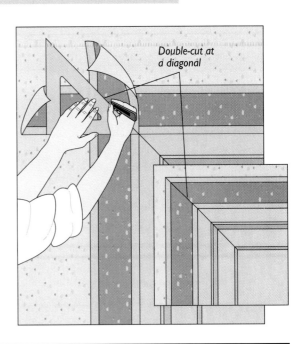

Double-cut at a diagonal

Caring for Wallpaper

The first step to ensuring long life and easy maintenance for your wallpaper is to choose a material suited to the room. Be especially careful in kitchens and bedrooms where walls are subject to heavy wear.

Before you buy, note the pros and cons of the different wallpaper materials available. See page 90 for a more detailed look at your choices.

As you hang wallpaper, be sure to wipe off excess adhesive from the walls and surrounding areas.

Protection: Applying a protective coating to a fabric or nonvinyl wallpaper lengthens its life and makes it easier to clean. Your dealer can suggest an appropriate coating. Before applying it, let the adhesive dry for about a week.

Wallpaper is especially vulnerable to damage at outside corners. A plastic corner guard or a strip of wood molding that you can stain or paint can prevent this problem.

Cleaning: Most wallpapers come with cleaning instructions. Test any cleaning product on a piece of scrap paper first. To remove dirt, try commercial wallpaper dough or kids' noncolored modeling clay. Clean washable paper with a solution of mild soap and water. Rinse with clear, cold water and dry with an absorbent cloth.

On nonwashable paper, blot with a sponge moistened with a solution of mild soap and cold water. Then, blot with cold water and dry. A dealer can recommend a spot remover for stubborn stains.

Repair: Press a matched, pasted scrap lightly against the damaged area. Make an irregularly-shaped razor-cut through both coverings, then lift off the patch. Remove the damaged piece, repaste the patch if needed, and smooth it in place.

Inspecting and Caring for Materials

Before you purchase any wallpaper, take a sample square home. Rub the paper with a wet sponge to test for colorfastness. If the paper tears easily when wet, it will be difficult to work with so you may wish to consider another choice.

Wallpaper is readily available in double-roll bolts, but you also may find it in single or triple rolls—the more rolls per bolt, the less wastage. Don't buy too little since it may be difficult to get an exact color match if you need to buy more later on.

As soon as your wall covering arrives, inspect it carefully. First, check that the pattern numbers are correct and the same on all rolls. Every roll should also have the same run, or dye-lot, number.

Then, carefully unroll each roll and inspect its entire length. Flaws to look for include uneven ink, wrinkled edges, and poor registration—colors that don't fall within their outlines in the design. Lay two rolls next to each other on a worktable—the pattern on the left edge of one roll should match that on the right edge of the other roll.

Always check wallpaper for defects before cutting from the roll—even if it's defective, you won't be able to return it once it has been cut.

If you find any problems, talk with your dealer right away. If the problem is small and the pattern is in limited supply, you may be able to figure out a way to work around the flaw.

Store your wallpaper in a dry area, such as a closet, until you're ready to hang it. To avoid wrinkles, lay the rolls horizontally rather than on end. Don't place anything heavy on top of them.

Finishing with FABRIC

For creating unique, vibrant walls, nothing rivals fabric. In its many incarnations—from sumptuous moiré and classy suede to informal canvas—fabric provides all the color, pattern, and texture of wallpaper while also lending sound absorbency and a special soft warmth to a room. Fabric has the further added benefit of being relatively easy to hang. Step-by-step instructions for the three basic fabric-application techniques—over batting, gluing, and stapling—are all shown on the following pages. With the information provided, even the first-timer can achieve professional results. Just be sure to take accurate measurements and, most important, be patient. Fabric offers some unique design opportunities. By using the same fabric for walls, ceilings, and even draperies, pillows, and furniture slipcovers, you can unify a room or bring the styles of adjacent rooms together. Plus, fabric will maintain its appearance long after papers have faded. Photos in this and the opening chapter demonstrate the uniqueness of fabric. The steps that follow will help you bring this special style to your own home.

Redwood-colored fabric on the walls brings out the warmth of the wood furnishings in this sparingly decorated bedroom. The natural grain of wood is even captured in the fabric's pattern.

Working with Fabric

At once elegant and modern, walls covered with fabric bring color and vitality along with sumptuous texture to a room. Detailed instructions are given starting on page 136, but here is an introduction to the basic techniques.

APPLICATION TECHNIQUES

Before embarking on a fabric project, think carefully about the look you want to achieve as well as the amount of time and effort you're willing to spend on the project. With all three methods, you can remove the fabric when you tire of it and reuse it for pillows, curtains, or other projects.

Upholstered walls: Covering walls with batting and fabric is the most time-consuming of the techniques, but the finished product provides some additional benefits. The batting under the fabric cushions the walls, provides soundproofing and insulation, and gives the fabric a soft, luxurious appearance. Trim, usually double welt, is used to finish the edges.

The most suitable rooms for wall upholstery are those that don't receive heavy use—dining rooms, bedrooms, and living rooms. This technique is not recommended for kitchens and bathrooms, where grease and steam are problems.

Whether fabric is upholstered, pasted, or stapled, it can help accentuate a room's color and style. The natural grains in this den's predominant wood motif are complemented by deep-red wall fabric. Plush carpet below reflects the wall's texture and color accents.

When choosing fabric, consider carefully how it will fit into the overall decor of the room. The gold-lamé color scheme in this elegant room is represented in the wall fabric—a random, subtle pattern adds visual interest.

You can upholster the ceiling as well, but it's best to do so only in a small room—to prevent sagging, you'll need to stretch the fabric and anchor it in several places.

Test the wall to see if stapling will damage it. Small holes left by staples can be filled with paint or a coat of spackling compound if you decide to remove the fabric later. If the staples can't puncture the surface or they leave large holes and chip the wall, mount furring strips (usually 1-by-3 wood strips) to provide a good working surface.

Pasted walls: With this technique, you apply adhesive to the wall—not the covering. Pasted fabric is resistant to steam and can be eas-ily removed without causing dam-age to the wall; any paste residue left on the walls can be washed off.

This method has some draw-backs, however. Bumps, cracks, or other damage will be revealed, so walls should be as smooth as pos-sible. Also, use primer on colored walls so light-colored fabrics won't appear tinted.

Stapled walls: For this application, stitch together fabric panels and install the covers in a similar way as for upholstered walls. However, you don't have to use batting or place the staples quite so close together. Also, the technique for corners is easier. To simulate the appearance of upholstered walls and increase the insulating and soundproofing qualities of the wall, choose a quilt-ed type of fabric.

CHOOSING FABRIC

Before you commit to one fabric, consider both its appearance and its suitability for the task you have in mind. All three techniques require about the same amount of fabric; upholstered walls also require bat-ting. Here are some shopping hints:

Decorating and upholstery fabrics: These fabrics come in widths up to 60 inches and often are treated with stain and dust repellent. They're printed with pattern overlaps at the selvages, or edges, making it easy to match the pattern at seams.

Flat bed sheets: These are good for upholstering or stapling. They are economical and available in many colors and designs. To determine the size and number you'll need, use these finished dimensions: twin, 66 by 96 inches; double, 81 by 96 inches; queen, 90 by 102 inches; king, 108 by 102 inches.

Printed fabrics: Usually the print will be slightly off-grain, veering at an angle from the lengthwise and crosswise threads. If the misalignment is too noticeable, look for another fabric.

To check the fabric, fold it back a few inches along the horizontal grain, "wrong" sides together, aligning selvages. If the print runs evenly along the fold, it's fairly well aligned. If the print wanders across the fold, it's badly off-grain.

All-over designs: The pattern can help camouflage wall imperfections and uneven ceiling lines. This type also shows less soil than those with large, open-ground patterns.

Stripes, plaids, and large geometric patterns: Beginners beware—any application mistakes will be distractingly obvious.

Room size: Dark colors, large patterns, and heavy textures make a room seem smaller; light colors, small patterns, and smooth textures make it look larger.

Test it: Buy a yard or two of fabric to pin to the wall for a week. Is it right?

The newest trend in fabric-covered walls—fabric loosely hung from decorative curtain rods—makes a room appear more cozy. Bold florals adorn the walls of this sitting room; the color scheme is echoed in the floor rug.

Tools for Applying Fabric

For upholstering or stapling, the most important piece of equipment you'll need is a staple gun along with a box of ⅜-inch staples. An electric gun, available from a tool rental company, will help you work faster. Most electric guns are fairly thick at the head, making it difficult to staple close to ceiling lines and corners. Use a less bulky hand-held staple gun for this close work. A tack hammer will help for staples that don't penetrate deeply enough. Cardboard tack strips, available from upholstery shops, hold the stapled fabric and maintain sharp edges in corners. Buy enough to run the wall's height at all inside corners, except where you begin and end—no strip is used there.

Use an electric glue gun and hot-melt glue to attach trim to fabric edges and fabric glue or spray adhesive to cover faceplates.

When stapling along the ceiling line or below molding, you'll need a ladder. A sewing machine is helpful for stitching together lengths of fabric to make covers for walls. Use an iron to remove creases in fabric and to press seams open.

Other tools include a staple remover, fabric shears for cutting, a broad knife or metal straightedge, and a screwdriver. Tools for pasting are listed on page 144.

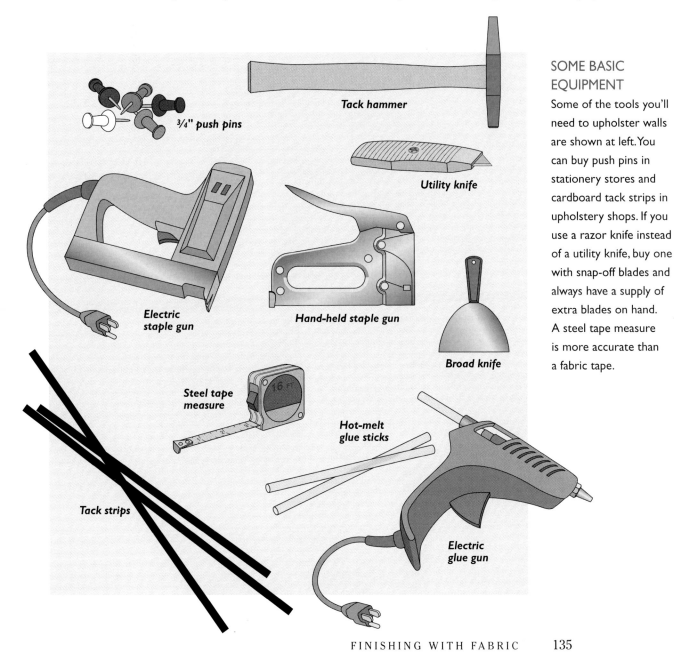

Tack hammer

¾" push pins

Utility knife

Electric staple gun

Hand-held staple gun

Broad knife

Steel tape measure

Hot-melt glue sticks

Tack strips

Electric glue gun

SOME BASIC EQUIPMENT

Some of the tools you'll need to upholster walls are shown at left. You can buy push pins in stationery stores and cardboard tack strips in upholstery shops. If you use a razor knife instead of a utility knife, buy one with snap-off blades and always have a supply of extra blades on hand. A steel tape measure is more accurate than a fabric tape.

Upholstering Walls

The steps for upholstering walls are simple: First, staple batting to the wall, then staple fabric covers—fabric panels seamed together—over the batting. Use a separate fabric cover for each wall. Finally, cover the staples and fabric edges with double welt or other trim.

DETERMINING YARDAGE

Check and recheck the yardage figures required for each material beforehand and buy enough to ensure you'll have ample material to complete the project. Your pattern or dye lot may not be available later if you need more supplies.

Measuring for fabric: Use a steel tape measure and mark dimensions—in inches—on paper. The figures will be used to determine yardage and cutting lines.

Measure the width of each wall you're planning to cover, unless you'll be working around an outside corner. In that case, one fabric cover will begin at one wall edge, wrap around the corner, and continue to the wall's far edge.

To find the number of fabric panels needed for a wall, divide wall width by the fabric's usable width. Seams take up room, too—allow half an inch for each seam.

If your result is a fraction, round up to the next whole number. The extra width allows you leeway to match the pattern at corners.

Next, measure the height of the same wall from the ceiling line or lower edge of the ceiling molding to the top of the baseboard. Take this measure in several places; use the largest of the figure variations.

Add 6 inches to the height as insurance against errors. If the fabric has a pattern repeat, add the

This bedroom, decorated with a French-country cotton motif, combines spirited hues and a lively mix of patterns. For color continuity, the walls are upholstered using the same fabric as the window and bed canopy. Companion borders and prints complete the coordinated look.
Design: Pierre Deux Original Fabrics

The deep-red fabric walls inject a broad swath of color to this den, bringing out the bright hues in the furnishings, curtains, and area rug.

repeat length to the height measurement to allow for matching the pattern at seams. The final figure is the working height of the wall.

For total fabric yardage, multiply the working-height figure by the number of fabric panels needed for the wall; divide this figure by 36 to convert to the number of running yards of fabric required for the wall.

Repeat the calculations for each wall you're covering. Add the yards for all the walls to determine total fabric yardage. Add extra yardage if you plan to trim the walls with double welt *(page 143)*. See page 139 to learn how to measure for trim.

Determining batting yardage: To pad the walls, use ¾-inch bonded polyester batting. Batting is available in stock 48, 54, or 96 inches wide and can be found in fabric stores or in home-furnishing or upholstery shops.

To compute the amount of batting, measure the exact width and height of the area to be covered. Total the widths of the walls and divide by batting width to determine the number of batting strips needed; round up to the next whole number. Multiply this figure by the wall's height and convert to yards to find the batting yardage needed.

Dimensions of large openings, such as sliding doors and picture windows, can be subtracted from the yardage figure since batting can be pieced around openings.

PREPARING FABRIC AND BATTING

With an all-over print, it's not necessary to plan where the seams will hang on the wall; once the fabric is stretched over the wall, the seams won't show. With a solid-color fabric, seams will be noticeable; plan their placement where they'll be least conspicuous. For a fabric with predominant motifs, center the pattern on the first wall.

Cutting the fabric: Spread the fabric on a flat, smooth surface. With tailor's chalk or a pencil, mark the point on the pattern that will lie along the ceiling line. From that point, measure down and mark the first strip's length according to the height measurement recorded.

Cut the fabric at the top and bottom markings. Continue cutting fabric panels, matching patterns, until there's enough to cover one wall. Panels should run in one direction—reversing the nap can produce color variations that may be seen only after the fabric is hung. Mark the top of each panel on the back of the fabric.

If a light-colored fabric has printing on the selvages, cut them off.

Pin together the panels you've cut for the first fabric cover before continuing. Be sure pattern placement at the top is the same for all subsequent fabric panels.

Stitching the seams: Pin the fabric panels together, matching the patterns at the edges. With ½-inch seam allowances, start at the top edge to stitch the panels; backstitch at the beginning and end of each seam. If you haven't trimmed the selvages, clip them every few inches so the seam allowances will lie flat. Press seams open and press out any creases with an iron.

Cutting the batting: Measure strips of batting in lengths equal to wall height. Cut enough strips to cover the entire area you're upholstering; fit the batting to width only when you staple it to the walls.

APPLYING BATTING, FABRIC, AND TRIM

Before you begin working, remove everything from the walls you are planning to upholster. Turn off the power to the room to prevent accidents when you're working around electrical openings. Work from left to right around the room; if you're left-handed, work from right to left. If you are upholstering the ceiling, do that before you cover the walls. Detailed step-by-step instructions for applying batting, fabric, and trim are provided starting on page 140. Here are some tips:

Hanging batting: With batting, it's best to start at the least conspicuous corner or at the edge of an opening that runs from floor to ceiling. Cut the batting ¾ inch away from the edges of all openings, except receptacles and switches. Since these will be covered with faceplates, carefully trim the batting just to the opening's edges.

Applying fabric covers: When stapling the first wall and centering a large motif, measure the distance from the center of the wall to the left corner, then measure the same distance on the fabric cover from the center of the motif to the left. Cut the fabric cover lengthwise at that point, being careful to cut exactly on the lengthwise grain.

Finishing the last wall edge: If you've worked around the room and have returned to the first wall, staple the last side to the first wall over the staples where you began.

FABRIC CARE

Fabric wall coverings are long-lasting and sturdy. With minimal maintenance, they will maintain their form, color, and style.

To prevent stains, treat the fabric with a stain repellent. You can buy repellent at a fabric or upholstery store and spray the fabric after installation—be sure to follow the manufacturer's instructions.

For normal, day-to-day cleaning, simply vacuum the walls as you would the floor. Ask your fabric dealer for advice if you encounter stubborn stains.

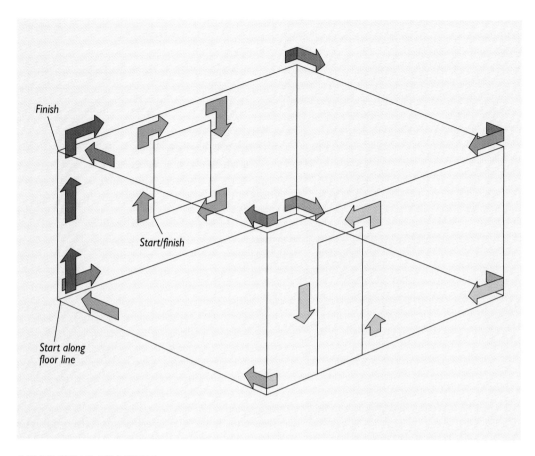

Finish

Start/finish

Start along
floor line

MEASURING FOR TRIM

Trim comes in many forms. For choices and installation instructions, see page 143. You should use a continuous strip of trim for the area's perimeter. To determine the amount of trim needed, start at an inconspicuous corner and measure the room along the floor (red arrows), moving around doors as shown. At the same starting point, measure up the corner of the wall and along the top at the ceiling line (blue arrows). Measure windows separately (green arrows). For total yardage, add the three numbers. Round up to the next half yard to give a margin of error.

Carefully cut away excess fabric with shears. Later, you'll glue trim over the staples to finish the edge.

If the final fabric side is along the edge of a floor-to-ceiling opening or corner, staple the fabric close to the wall's edge. Trim excess fabric with a utility or razor knife.

Covering narrow spaces: For wall strips narrower than 4 inches, cut poster board to fit the space; don't use batting. Wrap the fabric around the board and glue the edges in place on the back. With brads, tack the covered strip to the wall; poke nailheads under the fabric.

Covering faceplates: Use fabric glue for this purpose; you also can use spray contact cement, but it dries yellow so it's not suitable for light-colored fabrics.

Cut the wall-hung fabric along the edges of the electrical opening. Spread glue on the front of the face- plate, place it over the opening, then match the pattern of a fabric scrap to that on the wall.

Smooth the fabric to the face- plate's front, trim it to within a half inch of the edges, then cut away the corners and glue the overlap. Punch holes at the screw openings. Snip off loose threads.

Once everything is covered, you'll want to finish with trim. Turn to page 143 to learn how to do this.

Applying batting and fabric covers

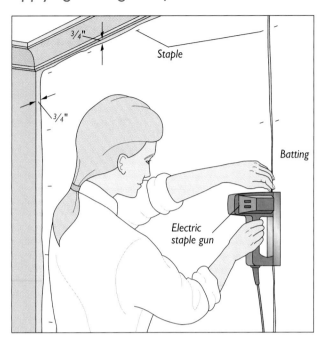

1 Positioning batting strips

Place the first batting strip ¾ inch away from the edges of the wall and ceiling or molding to allow space for stapling the cover. Staple the strip along the top, placing staples at least an inch from the batting edge and about a foot apart. Staple down the left side, then the right side of the batting. Cut any excess off the bottom edge, leaving a ¾-inch space at the baseboard; staple across the bottom. Butt the second batting strip against the first and staple it in the same way *(left)*. Continue until the area is covered. Stop batting ¾ inch from an inside corner; wrap batting around outside corners as for wallpaper *(page 113)*.

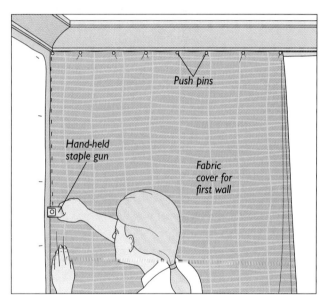

2 Applying fabric to the first wall

Pin the fabric along the ceiling line or molding edge for 3 to 4 feet. Then, starting at the top corner, staple the left side of the fabric to the wall *(right)*, positioning staples parallel to the wall edge and one staple-width apart.

3 Completing the first wall

Return to the top edge and staple the fabric held with push pins *(left)*. Then, with the remaining fabric in your right hand, fully extend your arm to the right and staple the fabric in place at that point. Repeat the procedure to the end of the wall. For outside corners, continue stapling, pulling the fabric tightly around the corner.

Check that the seams are straight: Hang a plumb line down the rightmost seam *(page 102)*. Pull the fabric taut at the bottom edge to straighten the seam, then staple the fabric's lower edge at the seam line. Finally, check the seams to the left—they should be straight. Staple each seam's lower edge in place.

4 Stapling an inside corner

Stretch the fabric around the inside corner and staple it to the second wall from top to bottom as far into the corner as possible *(right);* use staple-gun pressure and your hand to pull the fabric taut to the wall. Place staples parallel to the corner edge; be sure not to catch batting in the staples—which will create ridges in the finished wall.

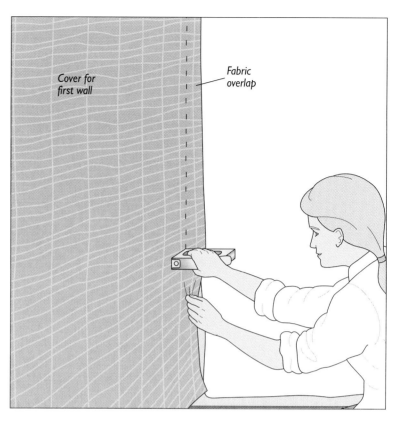

Cover for first wall

Fabric overlap

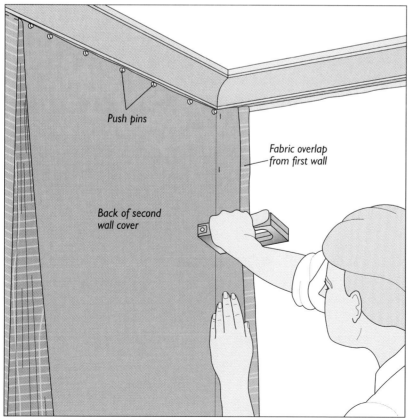

Push pins

Fabric overlap from first wall

Back of second wall cover

5 Covering the second wall

Pin the fabric cover for the second wall along the top edge of the first wall with the right (patterned) sides together. To match patterns, align the edge of the second cover to the pattern of the first one. Use the vertical line in the pattern or the fabric grain to ensure a pattern match all the way down the wall.

Staple the second fabric cover at several points in the corner on the second wall *(left);* as you staple, remove push pins and flip the fabric over to check pattern alignment. To make adjustments, remove staples and trim excess fabric.

6 Placing tack strips

Push a tack strip tightly into the corner on the second wall. Staple the strip to the wall over both fabric layers (right). The strip will hold the fabric in place and make a smooth, flat corner edge.

Next, butt a second tack strip to the bottom of the first and staple it in place. Apply additional strips, if necessary; use fabric shears to trim the bottom strip to fit.

Finally, remove the push pins, bring the second fabric cover over to the second wall so the patterned side is showing, and pin it 3 to 4 feet along the top edge.

Tack strip

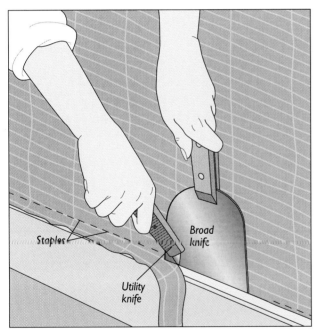

Stapler

Broad knife

Utility knife

7 Trimming the bottom edge

Staple the bottom edge of the first fabric cover as close to the baseboard as possible. Using a broad knife or straightedge to protect the fabric, carefully trim excess fabric along the top of the baseboard with a utility or razor knife (left). Keep the blade flat against the wall; change blades frequently to avoid pulling or stretching the fabric edges.

8 Working around openings

For doors and other openings hidden under the fabric, staple the fabric to the wall as close to the casing as possible (right), starting at the bottom edge. As you staple, cut holes for doorknobs and casing corners in order to keep the fabric taut. Finally, use a utility or razor knife to cut the fabric along the casing, protecting it with a broad knife or straightedge.

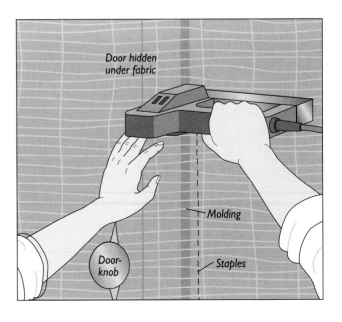

Door hidden under fabric

Molding

Door-knob

Staples

Many trims can provide a professional finish to your project. Double welt, made of the same fabric as that on the wall or of a complementary fabric, is common. You also can use heavy grosgrain ribbon, braid, gimp, or fabric-wrapped, stained, or painted molding. All are sold at fabric shops. For a different effect, try a contrasting color.

Double welt: This is the professionals' choice to cover staples and fabric edges decoratively. Measure the amount of welt needed as you would other trim *(page 139)* and make one continuous strip, then glue the welt into place *(below)*. When upholstering the entire room, apply welt along the baseboard, up the corner where you began, and along the top edge, using separate strips for each.

Buy ¼-inch piping cord twice the length of the trim measurement. Make the cord casing from strips of fabric cut on the bias, gathering enough 1¾-inch-wide bias strips to make a welt equal to the trim measure. Buy one yard of 45-inch-wide fabric for every 23 yards of welt. Buy one yard of 54-inch-wide fabric for every 28 yards of welt.

Ribbon, braid, or gimp: Apply these using the same technique as double welt. Work quickly when using hot-melt glue to attach grosgrain ribbon or the glue will harden and leave a ridge. If the braid is too bulky to turn under, cut the edge so it butts against the first braid end. Use fabric glue to keep edges from fraying.

Molding: Molding can be painted, stained, or covered with fabric. To cover with fabric, wrap fabric around the molding, glue the edges in place on the wrong side, and tack the molding to the wall at the edge of the fabric cover with brads.

Making and applying double-welt trim

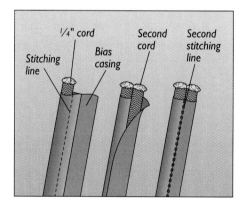

1 **Making double welt**
Cut enough bias strips to make a continuous welt and stitch the strips together using a sewing machine equipped with a zipper foot. Leave a ¼-inch seam allowance. Wrap one edge of the casing around a piece of piping cord, leaving a ⅛ to ¼-inch fabric flap *(far left)*.

Stitch close to the cord along the casing's entire length. Place the second piece of cord on the wrong side of the fabric next to the stitching line. Wrap the cover over the second cord *(middle left)*, then turn the welt to the front.

Using the sewing machine's regular presser foot, stitch over the first stitching line *(near left)*; hold the fabric securely so the cords are bound tightly together.

1 **Applying double welt**
With an electric glue gun, apply a 12-inch-long strip of hot-melt glue to the underside (side with raw edge) of the welt along the center stitching line. Place the welt along the bottom edge of the fabric cover a few inches from the corner with the raw edge facing the baseboard. Tack the trim with push pins *(right)*. Repeat the procedure for the next section of welt.

To work around corners, press the welt firmly and tightly into place with a screwdriver. Use long push pins to hold the welt until the glue dries.

To finish the ends along the baseboard or top edge, cut the welt 1 inch longer than the area remaining to be covered. Push the welt fabric back to expose both cords; cut an inch off the end of each cord. Next, fold the welt fabric ½-inch to the wrong side and coat it with fabric glue. Apply the remaining welt to the wall, letting the cordless fabric overlap the end of the welt.

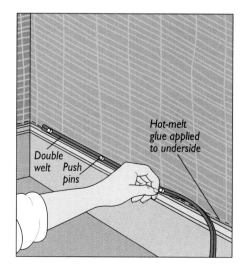

Pasting Fabric on Walls

Pasting fabric is recommended only for smooth, light-colored walls. Even so, choose your fabric carefully: Light colors with all-over patterns are best. Those that have a nap or are porous, such as velvet or wool, are not suitable. Nor are dark fabrics—adhesive can stain the fabric and dark dyes can bleed onto the wall.

Border fabric can be pasted on top of fabric walls as a trim after the walls are completely dry. When pasting panels, be careful not to drip adhesive onto them.

To paste fabric, clean the walls well and let them dry. If the walls have never been painted or are a dark color, apply a primer. Then, simply apply adhesive to each wall, a small section at a time. Finally, smooth down the fabric panels.

To remove pasted fabric, start from a corner along the baseboard and gently peel the fabric from the wall; the adhesive will come off as well. Using a damp sponge, wash the wall to remove any residue.

Tools and supplies: A plumb line, paint roller, utility or razor knife, and a broad knife or metal straightedge are essential tools for the job. You'll also need vinyl wallpaper adhesive, a large sponge, a paint tray for the adhesive, drop cloths to cover the floor, fabric shears, and ¾-inch push pins.

Preparation: Calculate the amount of fabric needed for the project as for any of the other application techniques *(page 136)*. Don't forget to deduct the selvage width that must be trimmed before the panels are joined on the wall.

Measure and cut fabric panels, allowing for an extra 2 inches or so at the top and at the bottom as a margin of error.

Protect the fabric with a broad knife or metal straightedge while cutting the selvages using a utility or razor knife.

Things to remember: Work fabric around corners, openings, and fixtures using the same techniques as for wallpaper *(page 112)*. When taking a break, place adhesive and brushes in plastic bags in the refrigerator so they don't dry out.

For tears, stains, or other damage, repaste the area and pat a matching piece of fabric into place. When the adhesive dries, cut off any loose fabric threads with a utility or razor knife.

For bubbles, brush adhesive on the fabric's front until it lies flat. Brush adhesive on wrinkles, then smooth the wrinkles away using your fingernail. In both cases, wipe the surface with a damp sponge before the adhesive dries.

Applying fabric with paste

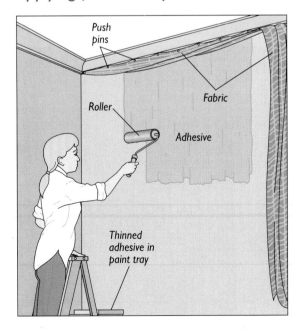

Push pins

Fabric

Roller

Adhesive

Thinned adhesive in paint tray

Pasting fabric

Establish plumb *(page 102)* and align the pattern along the top edge, leaving a 2-inch overlap. Tack the fabric at the top and adjust it to the plumb line, then tack it off to one side. Thin adhesive with water to the consistency of cream soup, then apply it to the wall with a paint roller *(left)* or brush, starting at the top and pasting down a few feet. Cover an area a few inches wider than the fabric's width. Remove the push pins from the side and lightly smooth the fabric into place with your hands. Work from the center out; don't stretch the fabric. Paste down loose threads or cut them—don't try to pull them out.

Tack and glue the rest of the wall, working one section at a time. Butt panel edges together so patterns match easily and seams won't shrink when dry. Apply adhesive to the fabric overlaps at the top and baseboard edges. Let the fabric dry for at least 24 hours, then trim the overlap with a utility or razor knife; protect the fabric with a broad knife or straightedge.

Stapling Fabric to Walls

Stapling fabric is the simplest, fastest way to add color and design to walls. Just measure and prepare the fabric covers *(page 136)*, then staple them to walls following the same progression as for upholstered walls *(page 140)*: left side, top edge, right side, and bottom.

Corners of stapled walls are easy to handle *(below)*. Stretch the fabric for the first wall to the corner and staple it to the first wall as far into the corner as possible.

Cover the staples and raw edges with trim *(page 143)*. To determine trim length, see page 139. Remember to add twice the wall height to your total for each corner—you need to cover the raw edges and staples on both sides of every corner.

For stapling to walls, you'll need a staple gun along with a large box of ⅜-inch staples (½-inch staples for quilted fabrics). Also have on hand a steel tape measure, fabric shears, a utility or razor knife, a broad knife or metal straightedge, a staple remover, and a ladder. Stitch the fabric panels, right sides together, with your sewing machine.

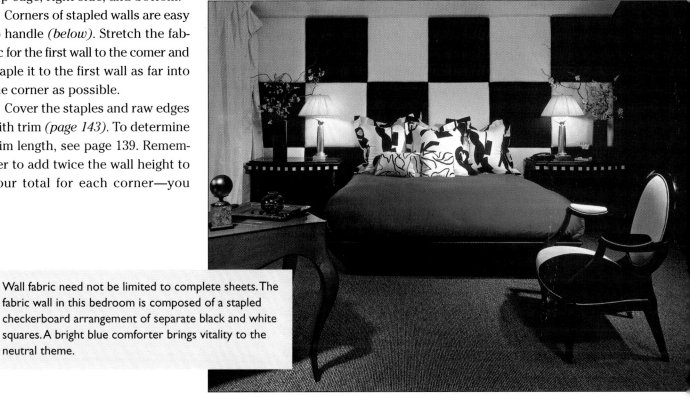

Wall fabric need not be limited to complete sheets. The fabric wall in this bedroom is composed of a stapled checkerboard arrangement of separate black and white squares. A bright blue comforter brings vitality to the neutral theme.

Stapling walls and corners

First wall

Second wall

Both sides of corner stapled

Stapling along baseboard

Stapling fabric

Staple fabric into both sides of corners as well as along the ceiling or molding and the baseboards *(left)*, placing staples 2 to 3 inches apart. To work around openings, see page 142. For more detailed instructions on stapling fabric to walls, refer to Steps 2 to 8 on pages 140 to 142.

Exterior PAINTING

No matter how perfect your lawn and landscaping or how colorful and well tended your garden, if the paint on your house is starting to peel or the colors are fading, the look of the entire property will suffer. Painting the exterior of a house is a big job, but if you take the time to do it properly the results will be well worth the effort. This chapter contains all the information you'll need to get the job done right. We begin by focusing on paint and primer options, then continue with a detailed section on diagnosing and solving a range of typical paint problems. You'll also get an overview of the tools required for the job and information on setting up ladders and scaffolding. A large percentage of any exterior painting project is preparation. We show you how to make repairs to exterior walls and how to prepare surfaces—by washing, scraping, and sanding—to ensure that paint will adhere well and produce a smooth, durable finish. Finally, you'll find step-by-step instructions and general information on effective painting techniques. The chapter ends with cleanup tips that help you remove any evidence of your work other than the professional-looking finish.

Crisp lines between siding and trim such as those on this house are the result of careful painting. Using the proper techniques will help ensure that you get this clean, neat appearance on your home's exterior.

Shopping for Paint and Stain

As with interior paint, there are essentially two kinds of exterior paints: alkyd, or oil-base, paint and latex, or water-base acrylic, paint. Primers, paints, and stains are available in both types.

LATEX VERSUS ALKYD

Alkyd and latex paints cure differently. Alkyd paints usually are dry to the touch in 4 to 6 hours and are dry to recoat in an overnight. Alkyds will continue to harden for several months after application but are sufficiently hard for use after 24 hours.

Latex paint usually is dry to the touch in a half hour and is resistant to light showers or dew after about 4 hours in warm, dry weather.

Exterior alkyd paints are available in two types: enamel and house paint. Enamel is generally available in a selection of shiny, ready-to-mix colors that are suitable for general-purpose use and particularly good for trim. Enamel paint dries to a hard, nonporous finish. Alkyd house paint is more flexible than enamel. It is not available in some states because of air-

quality regulations. In others, it is available only in quart cans, making it expensive to use as a coating for exterior siding.

The best exterior latex paint is made with all-acrylic resin. Lower-quality varieties are made with vinyl acrylic and other blends. While all-acrylic paints are more expensive, they offer very good adhesion, gloss, and color retention. The water-based formulation of latex paints makes them easier to clean up, less expensive, and faster drying than alkyds. In addition, latex paint dries

EXTERIOR FINISHES

The chart at right contains recommended primers and finishes for outdoor surfaces. In many cases, the use of a primer is not suggested—for a number of reasons. Wood doesn't need primer if it will be stained or painted with enamel. Vinyl or aluminum siding is sufficiently covered with two coats of acrylic latex. With brick, stucco, or concrete, the first latex finish coat performs the function of a sealer or primer, covering the surface without absorbing into the substrate.

PRIMERS AND FINISHES FOR EXTERIOR SURFACES		
SURFACE	**PRIMER**	**FINISH**
Wood or plywood siding	Alkyd	2 coats alkyd paint, flat/semigloss/gloss
	Latex	2 coats latex paint, flat/semigloss/gloss
	None	2 coats latex stain, solid hide
	None	2 coats alkyd stain, solid hide/semi-transparent
Hardboard siding	Alkyd	2 coats latex paint, semigloss/gloss
Wood trim	Latex	2 coats latex paint, semigloss/gloss
	Alkyd	2 coats alkyd paint, flat/semigloss/gloss
Wood deck	None	2 coats semi-transparent stain
	None	2 coats porch and floor enamel
Vinyl or aluminum siding	None	2 coats acrylic latex paint, flat/semigloss/gloss
Brick	None	2 coats latex paint, flat
Block	Latex block filler	2 coats latex paint, flat
Stucco	None	2 coats latex paint, flat
Concrete	None	2 coats latex paint, flat
Ferrous metal	Metal primer	2 coats alkyd paint, gloss
Galvanized metal	Galvanized metal primer	2 coats alkyd paint, gloss

The use of stain and paint on different sections of this home gives it a distinct country style. Staining the door along with the door and window trim highlights the natural wood grain to stunning effect.

Stucco walls are best covered with two coats of flat latex paint. On smooth walls like these, rollers—typically used for interior painting—can make short work of the job (but should be equipped with a thick nap).

to a porous finish, allowing moisture in the wood to evaporate through the paint film without causing peeling. The release of moisture from below paint is one of the leading causes of paint failure *(page 152)*.

On the other hand, alkyd paints tend to adhere better to problematic and glossy surfaces. And since alkyd paints dry more slowly than latex paints, brush and roller marks have time to flow out, leaving a smoother surface finish.

Whether you choose alkyd or latex, flat (nongloss) paint typically is used on siding as well as any part of the house exposed to moisture, while semigloss or gloss paint is well suited to trim and moldings for a contrast of texture and to doors because of their durability.

STAINS AND VARNISHES

Stains come in transparent, semitransparent, and solid-hide formulations. Solid-hide stains are used on wood siding and fences. Semitransparent stains also are used on wood siding and fences, as well as on decks. Transparent formulations are used only on cedar or redwood (naturally rot-resistant woods) since they offer little protection against weathering and have poor hiding on previously-stained surfaces.

Varnishes need constant maintenance if used on surfaces exposed to direct sunlight. Choose a varnish with UV (ultraviolet) inhibitors to protect the wood. A base of four or five coats is recommended—with annual recoating not unusual.

See the chart on page 148 to match paints, primers, and stains with different surfaces.

High-gloss paints are appropriate for railings since they stand up well to wear and tear.

Paint Failure

It's important to take a close look at damage to the existing paint cover. From the symptoms of paint failure you can determine the causes and take action to avoid or reduce the problem in the future.

Daily exposure to the elements eventually takes its toll on all exterior painted surfaces. However, additional factors, including poor surface preparation, incompatible paints, or sloppy application can accelerate the process.

Depending on the symptoms presented, some surfaces may need to be stripped bare while others may require no more than a light sanding or scraping. When in doubt, clear the surface of all old paint. And if you are planning to repaint indoors, note that some of the conditions shown on the following pages also can occur on interior surfaces.

DIAGNOSING AND SOLVING EXTERIOR PAINT AND STAIN PROBLEMS

Dye and resin bleeding through finish

Redwood, cedar, and cypress contain water-soluble material that can bleed through latex products, resulting in unsightly stains on the surface of the paint finish *(left)*. Use of an alkyd primer can reduce the chance of bleeding. Softwoods such as pine can contain excessive amounts of pitch or sap—especially in knots—that may bleed through finish paints. Prime knots with orange shellac before painting.

Stain peeling from wood deck

Decks often are stained or painted after construction. This leaves the bottom and sides of planks unfinished, allowing moisture to enter the wood. As coating thickness increases with additional applications of stain, moisture causes adhesion failure *(right)*. To prevent this, stain (or paint) all sides and end grain prior to assembling the deck or finish the underside as well as top surfaces after assembly.

Multiple-coat peeling

Older buildings that have been painted many times, especially with oil-based paints, will sometimes experience paint failures that reveal bare wood *(left)*. As the paint thickness increases and the paint ages, the combined paint film becomes brittle and cracks as the wood below shifts due to humidity and temperature changes. Eventually, moisture enters through the cracks and causes peeling. The treatment is to strip the surface back to bare wood and treat it as new wood.

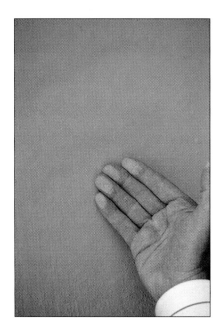

Chalking

Chalking *(left)* is the normal breakdown of a paint finish after long exposure to sunlight. The recommended treatment is to wash off the loose, powdery material and repaint.

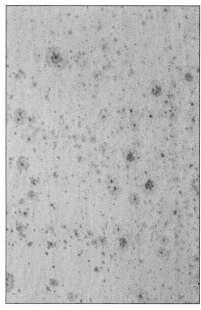

Grain cracking on plywood

When plywood is repeatedly exposed to moisture, the surface will develop small cracks as the wood expands and contracts *(right)*. Once cracked, repair usually isn't possible. The recommended treatment is to replace the plywood. Prime new plywood with an exterior-grade primer followed by at least two coats of alkyd or latex finish to provide adequate film thickness for protection.

Mildew

Mildew primarily is caused by a fungus that grows on cool, damp, shaded surfaces, showing up as black spots *(above)*. The recommended treatment is to wash the affected area with a solution of TSP (trisodium phosphate), detergent, household bleach, and warm water. Here is a standard recipe that can be adjusted to the size of your job: $2/3$ cup TSP, $1/3$ cup detergent, 1 quart bleach, 3 quarts warm water. Wear rubber gloves and eye protection when applying the solution.

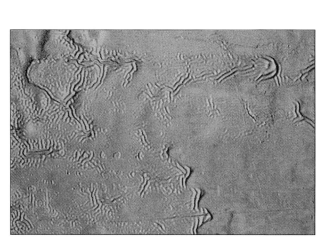

Wrinkling

Wrinkling *(left)* is caused by applying a coat of paint over another that isn't thoroughly dry. It also can occur if a single application is applied too heavily. The recommended treatment is to allow the paint to dry thoroughly, sand off the wrinkles, and repaint.

Inter-coat peeling

The use of latex finish coats over surfaces previously painted with gloss alkyd often results in poor adhesion *(right)*. The recommended treatment is to sand off the latex paint, prime the surface with an alkyd primer, and then apply latex finish coats. (Some top-of-the-line acrylic paints can be applied over old alkyd paint without priming, but thorough sanding is required first to give the surface "bite.")

Peeling varnish

Even the best exterior-grade spar varnishes do not last more than a few years before they start breaking down with exposure to sunlight *(left)*. The recommended treatment when varnishing exterior wood is to apply a minimum of 5 coats in the first application, followed by a light sanding and an additional coat every year. Maximum exposure before revarnishing is 2 years.

Peeling from galvanized metal

When an alkyd paint is applied to galvanized surfaces without a galvanized-metal primer being applied beforehand, a loss of adhesion will eventually occur *(left)*. The recommended treatment is to remove all the alkyd paint, prime, and apply new finish coats. (Some acrylic latex paints can be applied directly onto galvanized surfaces—ask your paint dealer.)

Efflorescence

Efflorescence is a white, powdery material that is formed as moisture moves through masonry surfaces. Eventually the combination of efflorescence and moisture will cause even latex paints designed to "breathe" to peel *(left)*. Efflorescence can be scrubbed off and rinsed away with water. In extreme cases, you may need to use muriatic acid. Consult a masonry supply store for directions and safety guidelines. The recommended treatment is to find the moisture source and repair it before repainting.

Peeling on window sills

Properly designed sills slope away from the window to prevent water pooling on the surface. However, this is not always the case, making window sills particularly susceptible to paint failure. Moisture eventually finds its way into the wood, causing peeling *(right)*. Cracks develop in the wood that further aid the entry of moisture. The recommended treatment is to sand to bare wood, prime with alkyd primer, fill cracks with paintable caulk, and apply two coats of finish paint.

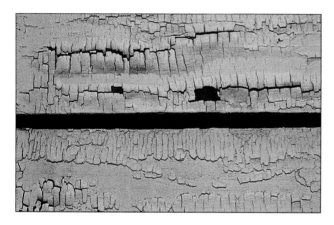

Alligatoring

Alligatoring *(above)* can be caused buy applying a hard finish coat over a soft primer. It also can be caused by the loss of flexibility of thick layers of paint on wood surfaces. The recommended treatment is to remove all the old paint by scraping and sanding. Repaint with a primer and two finish coats.

Blistering

Blistering *(above)* can be caused by moisture in the surface under the paint film. Common sources of moisture are lack of a vapor barrier in older homes, cracked boards, and poor caulking. Blistering also can be caused by solvent trapped in oil-based paints when using dark colors in hot weather. In either case, scrape and sand the blistered paint and eliminate any sources of moisture in the wall. Repaint in cool weather.

Lap marks

If you don't keep a wet edge as you stain or paint, lap marks *(left)* may develop where wet and partially dry material overlap during application. The recommended treatment is to stain or paint only two or three boards at a time, going from top to bottom on vertical siding, from side to side on horizontal siding.

Selecting the Right Tools

The tools that you need to accomplish a professional-level exterior-painting job are more extensive than you might imagine. This is because in addition to the obvious items—such as a few good paint-brushes—you'll need tools to prepare the surfaces and in many cases to make repairs as well.

All surfaces to be painted should at the very least be washed. For this, you'll require a bucket and scrubbing brush, along with gloves and safety goggles to protect yourself from the cleaning solution. You will need the same protective gear as well as a dust mask for other parts of the job such as sanding.

Scrapers and sanders are essential for removing loose paint—or, when necessary, an entire finish. A

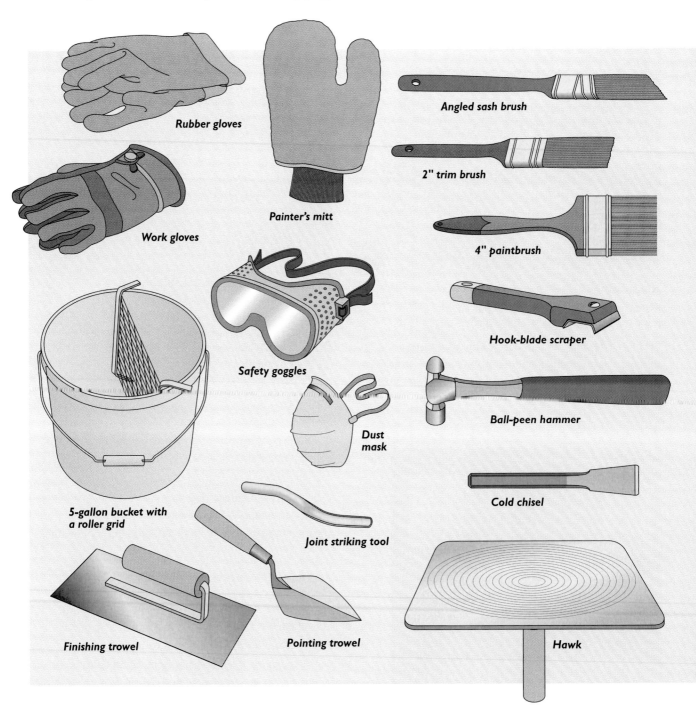

Rubber gloves

Painter's mitt

Angled sash brush

2" trim brush

4" paintbrush

Work gloves

Safety goggles

Hook-blade scraper

Dust mask

Ball-peen hammer

5-gallon bucket with a roller grid

Cold chisel

Joint striking tool

Finishing trowel

Pointing trowel

Hawk

disk sander, which you may choose to rent if you don't own one, is particularly useful for more extensive sanding jobs. To smooth the rough edges of small scraped areas, you can use an electric drill with a rotary sander attachment.

The tools that you'll need to repair surfaces will of course vary according to the surface and the nature of the repair. Repairing cracks in masonry walls requires a selection of standard masonry tools, including a ball-peen ham-mer and a cold chisel. Replacing a section of siding requires a back-saw to cut out the damaged piece and in the case of board siding, tools to patch the repair.

For information on choosing a paintbrush, turn to page 38.

Putty knife

Backsaw

Hand brush

Electric drill

Heat gun

Disk sander and sanding disks

Wire brush attachment

Molding scraper

EXTERIOR PAINTING TOOLS

The selection of tools shown at left will get you through most exterior painting jobs. Don't scrimp on quality when purchasing brushes. It is one instance where higher quality defi-nitely yields better results. When painting a masonry surface that needs repairs, you'll also require a finish-ing trowel, pointing trowel, joint striking tool, ball-peen hammer, cold chisel, and hawk, as shown at the bot-tom of the opposite page.

Cleaning Surfaces

Paint will not adhere properly to dirty surfaces. All painted exterior surfaces that will receive a new coat should be washed with a solution of trisodium phosphate (TSP), bleach, and warm water. TSP is a cleaning agent available in powdered form at most hardware stores. To mix the solution, follow the directions on the label. Because the solution is caustic, it is not intended for bare wood or masonry walls.

Before washing surfaces, cover plants close to the house with plastic tarps to protect them from splattering (and be sure to uncover them as soon as you've finished washing to avoid suffocating them). Protect yourself by wearing safety goggles and rubber gloves.

At the same time, cover stone and brick walls and patios so they do not become discolored by contact with the cleaning solution.

Prepare bare wood by sweeping off loose dirt with a broom, working from top to bottom. If the wood has been exposed to the elements for more than a few weeks, sand it first to remove mold and mildew.

Washing surfaces by hand

1 Washing the surface
Wash a roughly 15-foot-wide section of the surface with a brush dipped in a TSP solution. Using generous quantities of the solution, sweep the brush across the surface *(left)*; hard scrubbing shouldn't be necessary.

2 Rinsing off with a hose
After washing the first section with the TSP solution, rinse it thoroughly with a garden hose, starting at the top and working down *(right)*. Repeat Steps 1 and 2 until all surfaces to be painted are clean. Let surfaces dry for one to two days before painting.

Cleaning with a Power Washer

Power washers are high-pressure cleaning tools that make short work of washing exterior surfaces. They are particularly useful for large jobs or for surfaces that are extremely dirty.

Available for purchase or rent at many paint and hardware stores, the power washers force water through a hand-held nozzle, allowing you to blast away dirt and loose paint. Most models have a separate reservoir for cleaning agents, which means that the same tool can be used for both cleaning and rinsing.

1 Washing the surface
Fill the washer with the cleaning solution recommended by the manufacturer. Holding the nozzle about 18 inches from the surface, squeeze the trigger and slowly spray back and forth across a section of the wall (left), *working from the top down. Repeat the process at 5- or 6-foot intervals.*

2 Rinsing the surface
Holding the nozzle closer to the surface (about 6 to 10 inches away), rinse thoroughly with fresh water. Once again, spray successive sections of the wall by moving the nozzle slowly back and forth (right), *moving from top to bottom.*

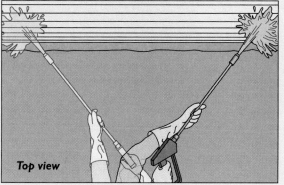

Top view

Preparing Surfaces for Painting

In many cases, simply washing the surface to be painted is not enough. Generally, paint that has begun to fail must be completely removed to ensure the new coat will adhere properly. While this is a big job, the reward for taking the time to prepare surfaces properly is a better-looking, longer-lasting paint job.

SCRAPING

To scrape small areas of peeling paint, a paint scraper, putty knife, or molding scraper all make useful tools. Even where a sander can be used to remove an entire finish, you will still need to scrape areas where the sanding wheel won't reach, such as corners and other tight spots.

To ensure you loosen as much paint as possible, scrape areas of loose paint from every direction; sometimes old paint scraped from left to right seems solid but comes off easily when scraped from the opposite direction. Use two hands on the scraper, keeping it flat to avoid gouging the wood. If you do create gouge marks, sand them down or fill them with vinyl patching compound so they don't show through the new paint job.

If the paint that remains after scraping has high or rough edges, sand, or "feather," them down with coarse sandpaper. This way they will be less noticeable once they have been painted over.

Other possibilities for removing paint are power sanders, discussed below, as well as heat guns and liquid paint strippers, discussed later in this section.

POWER SANDING

Power sanders can be used to smooth the edges of scraped areas or to clear an entire surface of paint *(facing page)*. For big jobs, an industrial 7-inch sander works well. Keep in mind that sanding is a demanding, noisy job that requires much care and concentration.

Sanding is done in two stages. First, the paint cover is completely removed with coarse sandpaper (60-grit paper is generally best). As coarse paper will leave cuts in the wood, the same area must then be smoothed with medium sandpaper (100 grit). Surfaces should be com-

To achieve a beautiful paint job like the one shown at left, surfaces must be free of loose paint, dirt, and debris. To ensure this, most surfaces will require scraping, sanding, and washing.

pletely free of paint before fine sandpaper is applied or the paper will become clogged quickly with softened paint.

If you have little sanding experience, you may find the process difficult to get used to and tiring. Sanders are heavy and powerful, and must be handled very carefully to prevent gouging siding. Make sure the sander is running at full speed before touching the wheel to the surface. As you bring the sander into contact with the wall, lean on it slightly until you hear the motor slow. The sanding wheel should be kept at a very slight angle (5 to 10 degrees) to the wall; otherwise, the wheel will spin out of control across the surface. Discard sanding disks as they become clogged with paint and begin to burn the surface.

Also remember that sanding is a noisy, messy business—and it can be dangerous. Protect yourself from flying paint chips, dust, noise, and the spinning disk of the sander with the proper safety equipment—ear plugs, a dust mask, safety goggles, gloves, and heavy work clothes.

Make sure the sander is turned off when you plug it in—or it could be sent flying.

Keep the sanding wheel well away from your body so it is less likely to nick you if it should happen to jump back unexpectedly.

Stay alert while sanding. The job can get boring, but if you let your attention wander you open yourself to the possibility of an accident.

Like other electrical devices, sanders should not be used in the rain. Exposing the sander or its extension cord to water can cause a short circuit.

Finally, never use a sander near flammable liquids, such as gasoline, paint thinners, or solvents. It may throw a spark and ignite the fluid.

Sanding and scraping clapboard siding

1 Sanding clapboard in sequence

Starting with coarse paper, sand successive 2- or 3-foot sections of single boards following the order shown in the numbered illustration above. Begin by pushing the spinning sanding wheel up against the lip of an overhanging board (left). Remove the paint along the lip (1), then sand each end of the first section (2). Sand the middle of the section by moving the sander in a wave-like pattern (3), then sand the bottom of the section (4). Finally, sand the underside of the lip (5, Step 2). Avoid pushing the sanding wheel all the way into corners so you have room to feather the edges of paint the sander can't reach (Step 3).

2 Sanding the underside of the lip

To sand the underside of the lip, hold the sander on its side with the wheel facing upward *(left)*. Once the surface is finished, sand it again with fine sandpaper to eliminate sander marks in the wood.

3 Feathering and scraping corners

Corners and some other areas cannot be fully reached by the sander. Feather the edges between paint and wood using the sander fitted with coarse sandpaper. Next, scrape any loose paint out of the corners with a molding scraper *(right)*.

PREPARING SHUTTERS FOR PAINTING

If you have wooden shutters that need to be sanded and scraped prior to painting, it's best to remove them and do the work on the ground.

Look the shutters over carefully. If the louvers, or slats, are covered with thick layers of damaged paint, it may be worth having them stripped professionally. With professional chemical treatment, shutters will come back virtually free of old paint, leaving you to simply prime and repaint.

However, if you really want to prepare shutters yourself, you can work on them in the garage or shed on rainy days when you're obliged to take a break from your outdoor chores.

Label each shutter to remind you which window it belongs with (shutters can differ slightly in size) and remove all screws or nails from the shutters. When it's time to put the shutters back up, use new hardware.

When you inspect the shutters, you may discover loose louvers or frames. Tighten a loose louver with a wooden wedge 1 to 2 inches in length inserted between the louver and the frame. Cut the wedge to size with a coping saw. Pull one end of the loose louver out of the frame, apply wood glue on the ends of the louver and wedge, and lightly tap the wedge into place with a hammer. Allow the glue to cure for 24 hours.

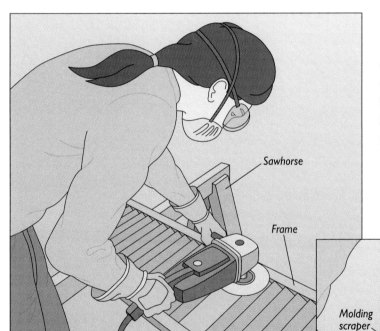

Sawhorse

Frame

Molding scraper

Louver

1 Sanding the shutter frame
Place the shutter on a sturdy workbench or across two sawhorses. Sand the frame with coarse sandpaper. Follow this with a second sanding using fine sandpaper. On the louvers, a single light pass with coarse paper will be sufficient to remove loose paint and to smooth edges *(left)*.

2 Scraping corners
The corners between the frame and the louvers are particularly prone to peeling. Scrape each joint free of loose paint using a molding scraper *(right)*.

IRON RAILINGS

Iron railings are attractive and sturdy, but very prone to rusting. If you have an iron railing and are painting other surfaces close by, paint the railing as well. It will make the whole job look a lot better.

Remove rust and loose paint before painting. This is best done using an electric drill with a wire brush attachment. A wire brush can then be used to clear rust and paint from harder-to-reach spots. Both techniques are shown below.

Once the railing is prepared, coat it right away with a high-quality rust-inhibitive metal primer. Leaving metal surfaces unprotected for as little as a day can result in rust reappearing. Then, paint the railing with an alkyd gloss enamel.

You can paint with a brush or with a painter's mitt as shown on page 185. Spray paint also can be used, but it tends to be expensive.

Preparing an iron railing for painting

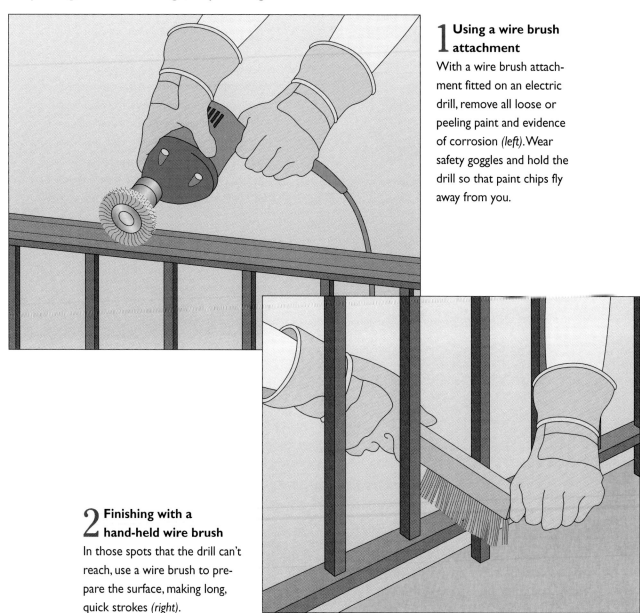

1 Using a wire brush attachment
With a wire brush attachment fitted on an electric drill, remove all loose or peeling paint and evidence of corrosion *(left)*. Wear safety goggles and hold the drill so that paint chips fly away from you.

2 Finishing with a hand-held wire brush
In those spots that the drill can't reach, use a wire brush to prepare the surface, making long, quick strokes *(right)*.

164

While scraping and sanding are the most commonly used methods for removing old paint and preparing surfaces, a number of other options are available that can be useful in certain situations.

Liquid paint remover: Sometimes ornate woodwork can be difficult to prepare for painting by scraping or sanding, or it may be damaged if you try. A useful solution may be to use liquid paint remover.

By applying paint remover to a painted surface, the chemicals in the product break down the bond between the paint and the surface, causing the paint to bubble and soften. It can then be removed gently from the surface with a putty knife or paint scraper.

Liquid paint removers are caustic so you should use them only outside in good ventilation. Always wear rubber gloves and safety goggles since contact with the skin can cause burns that leave scars and contact with the eyes can be very harmful.

Heat guns: To remove especially tenacious areas of paint, a heat gun can be useful *(below)*. Heat guns, though, can be dangerous; they function at extremely high temperatures and can easily ignite any flammable material—such as sawdust or paper—they contact.

Removing paint with a heat gun

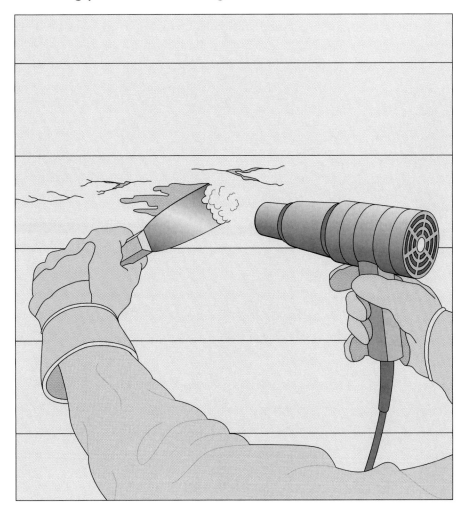

Using a heat gun
Hold the heat gun several inches from the surface. As the paint begins to bubble and melt, scrape it off with a putty knife or scraper *(left)*.

Repairing Damaged Surfaces

In time, even the best-maintained homes begin to show signs of deterioration. As you wash and prepare surfaces, take note of any damage since it will have to be repaired before you paint. This section provides instructions for repairing several types of siding, masonry walls, gutters and downspouts, flashing, and glazing putty on windows.

The most common problem you are likely to come up against is rotten wood, particularly on siding, but elsewhere as well. If damage of this kind is limited, you can dig out the bad wood with a scraper or old screwdriver and fill in the hole with caulk or other patching filler. Caulk is especially useful for small cracks and holes. But unlike fillers such as plastic wood, caulk can't be sanded so it should be applied as evenly and smoothly as possible.

If the damage is spread across an entire siding panel or there is not enough wood left to hold a repair, the entire section of siding will have to be replaced.

Before you repair any damage, determine the cause of the problem. Moisture is most often to blame. Leaking gutters, for example, can cause damage to walls. Inspect them before you paint. Leaks in the roof also are possible culprits. Check and repair flashing as necessary *(page 176)*.

When the source of moisture is not obvious, you should consider hiring a professional to find a solution. Remember, if you don't remedy the cause of the problem, the repaired surface will soon begin to disintegrate again.

If you plan to paint a masonry wall, the kinds of repairs that may be required will be quite different. Typically, these jobs will involve repointing damaged mortar joints in brick walls and repairing cracks in concrete walls (see pages 173-175).

Before you can apply an immaculate paint job such as the one shown at left, you may need to do some repairs—from replacing siding boards to repairing gutters.

The most common repair you'll need to tackle on the exterior of windows is replacing old glazing compound. Inspect the condition of the glazing compound before painting. It is supposed to form a waterproof seal between the glass and the window sash. If the glazing compound has hardened and chipped, cracked, or pulled away from the glass or sash, it needs replacing. If there are only very small cracks and the compound is still bonded to the glass and sash, you can paint over it.

If you need to replace the glazing compound, do so only after all sanding and scraping have been completed. If you do it before, the new compound will quickly be covered in dust and will need to be replaced all over again.

Replacing glazing compound

1 Removing old putty
Wearing goggles to protect your eyes, use the point of a molding scraper to remove old glazing putty from the window sashes *(right)*.

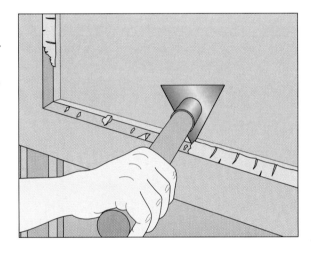

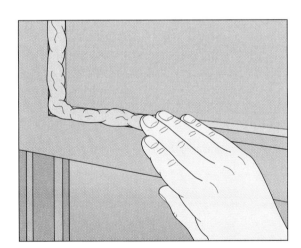

2 Applying glazing compound
Brush the sash with an old paintbrush to remove dust. If any glazier's points are missing, replace them. Press glazing compound along the sash with your hand so it is spread evenly *(left)*.

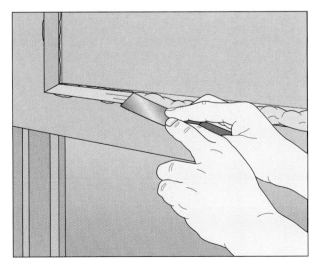

3 Smoothing the putty
Hold a putty knife at a 30-degree angle to the glass and press the glazing compound into the corner, then pull the knife toward you *(left)*. Remove any excess with your hand, then run your finger gently along the compound in the opposite direction, making sure it sits flush against the glass and the sash. Let the compound set for at least a week before applying paint.

GUTTERS AND DOWNSPOUTS

Blocked or damaged gutters can cause water stains on a new paint job and eventually lead to bulging or flaking paint along the top of a wall just below the gutter.

Whether your gutters are made of aluminum, stainless steel, or wood, keep them free of debris and make sure downspout openings are clear. Remove obstructions from the openings with a stick or an old screwdriver. Clearing gutters will involve working from a ladder, so choose a dry, calm day for the job.

To check gutters for leaks and to verify that they drain properly, inspect them when it's raining or feed a garden hose into the gutter and turn it on. If you discover a leak in your gutters, repair it as shown below.

Repairing a leaking gutter

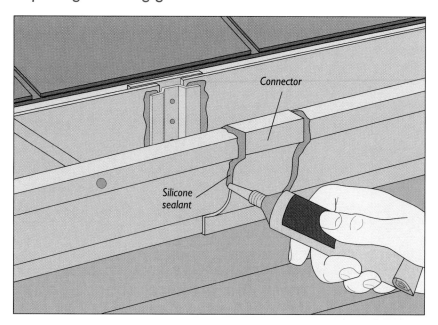

Connector

Silicone sealant

Sealing joints
Apply silicone sealant or caulk to the seams where the gutter sections and connector meet *(left).* Seal both the inside and the outside of the gutter.

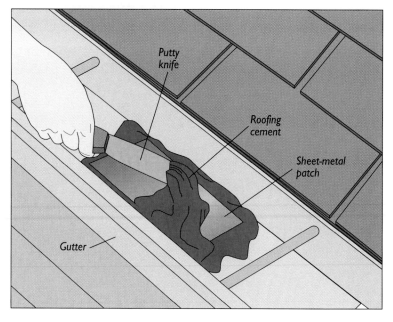

Putty knife

Roofing cement

Sheet-metal patch

Gutter

Sealing a hole
For a small hole, use a putty knife to apply a thin coat of roofing cement, extending the cement beyond the hole in all directions. For a hole larger than $1/2$ inch in diameter, apply roofing cement and embed a sheet-metal patch in it. Apply more cement over the patch, sealing the edges *(right).*

Siding is made from various materials, each of which requires specific repair techniques.

Wood siding: Wood siding is both attractive and durable, but requires regular maintenance. To prevent deterioration, repair simple surface problems as soon as possible—fill small holes in the wood with patching compound and fix split boards *(below)*. Boards that are badly damaged will need to be replaced following procedures shown on the next few pages. First, determine and remedy the cause of any serious damage. Moisture may be the culprit. Check for deteriorating roofing as a possible source.

Aluminum siding: Aluminum siding panels that have been badly damaged should be replaced as shown on page 172. The following are some common minor repairs: To remove a dent, drill a hole into the center of it and drive in a self-tapping screw with two washers under the screwhead. Pull on the screwhead with pliers to bend back the siding. Remove the screw and fill the hole with aluminum filler, following the instructions on the product label. When dry, sand the filler smooth.

Repairing a split board

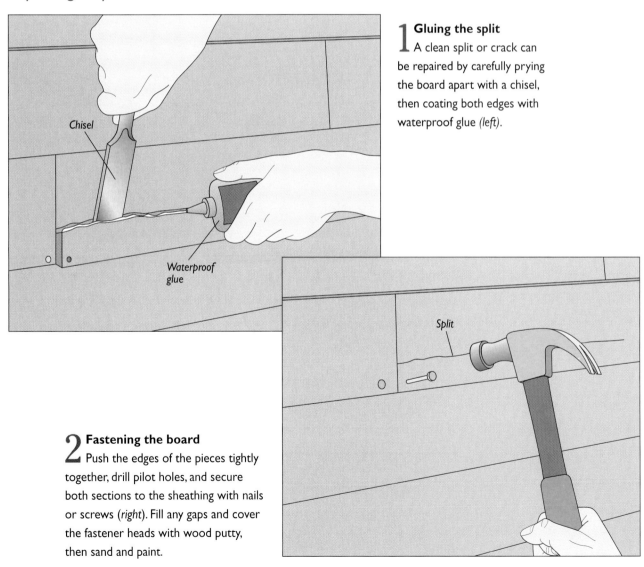

1 Gluing the split
A clean split or crack can be repaired by carefully prying the board apart with a chisel, then coating both edges with waterproof glue *(left)*.

Chisel

Waterproof glue

Split

2 Fastening the board
Push the edges of the pieces tightly together, drill pilot holes, and secure both sections to the sheathing with nails or screws *(right)*. Fill any gaps and cover the fastener heads with wood putty, then sand and paint.

Replacing a section of tongue-and-groove board

1 Removing the board
Because the boards are locked together by tongues and grooves, the damaged piece must be cut at each end and split lengthwise to be removed. (Shiplap and channel rustic siding also are replaced this way.) Pull out all nails in the section to be removed. Mark the end cuts, then make a series of passes across the board almost to the top and bottom of each line with a circular saw; set the blade depth just shy of the siding thickness. Carefully hold back the blade guard, then lower the moving blade into the wood to start each cut; finish the cuts with a chisel and a mallet. Cut along the center of the damaged section almost to the end cuts (*right, top*). Hold the saw firmly—it may kick back. Also be careful not to cut into adjacent boards. Cave in the board by pressing on it, then pull out the loosened pieces (*right, bottom*). Apply roofing cement to repair any cuts in the building paper.

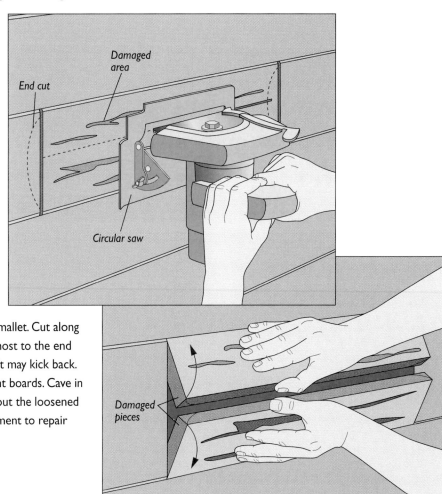

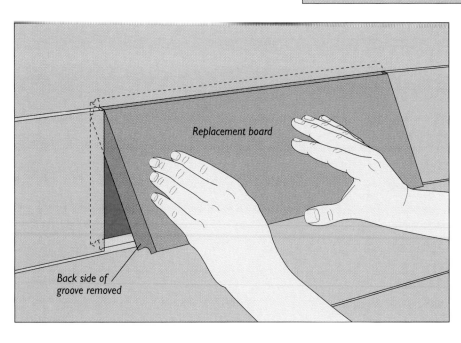

2 Installing a new board
Remove the backside of the groove on the replacement board, then slide it in place (*left*) and nail the board to the sheathing. Countersink the nailheads, caulk or putty the nail holes and end joints, and sand the board.

Replacing a piece of clapboard siding

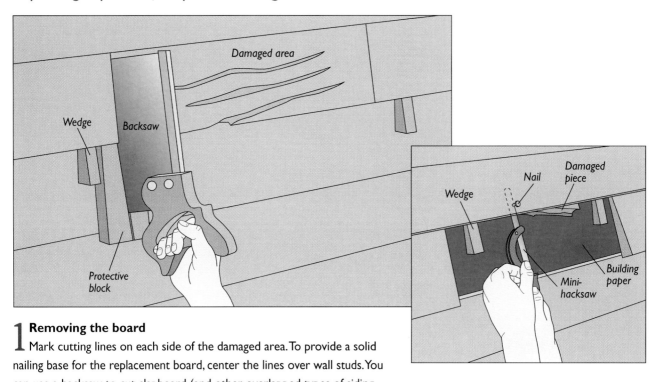

1 Removing the board

Mark cutting lines on each side of the damaged area. To provide a solid nailing base for the replacement board, center the lines over wall studs. You can use a backsaw to cut clapboard (and other overlapped types of siding such as bevel and Dolly Varden). Pull out nails in the way of your cuts. Pry up the bottom edge of the damaged board with a pry bar, then drive small wooden wedges underneath it at each end outside the cutting lines to keep it raised. Cut through the board along the cutting lines *(above)*; finish the cuts with a compass saw or a chisel and a mallet. Break out the damaged board—in pieces, if necessary. Pull out or cut remaining nails in the board with a mini-hacksaw, if necessary, to remove damaged bits *(inset)*. Repair any tears in the building paper with roofing cement.

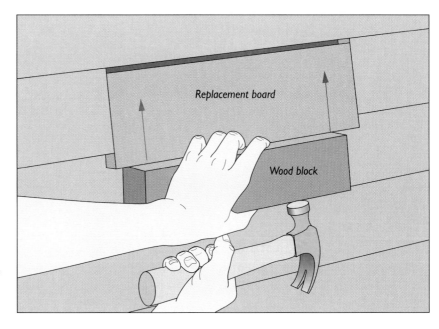

2 Installing a new board

Trim a replacement board to length and drive it into position by hammering against a wood block *(right)*. Nail the board's bottom edge to the sheathing. Caulk or putty the nail holes and board ends.

Replacing a section of plywood or hardboard siding

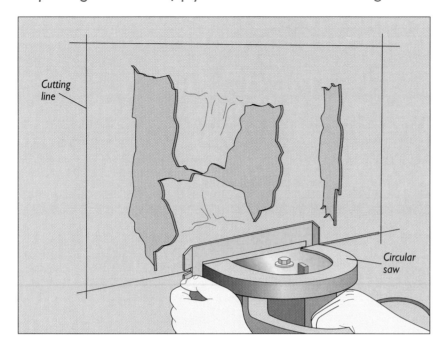

Replacing a damaged section
Mark the cuts to be made using a square for accuracy. Center the vertical cuts over studs. Cut out the damaged section with a circular saw *(left)*; use a hacksaw at the corners. Install 2-by-4s as backing where needed to support edges of the replacement piece. Patch any tears in the building paper with roofing cement. Cut a replacement piece and nail it in place. Caulk the nailheads and the seams.

Replacing aluminum siding

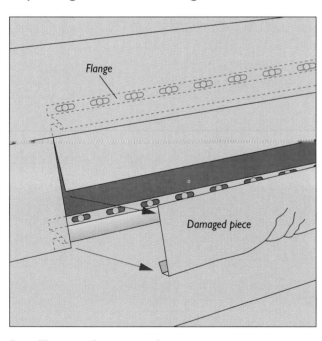

Installing a replacement piece
Cut through the center of the panel to points just past the ends of the damaged area using a utility knife. Make vertical cuts at each end and remove the lower part of the damaged section, leaving the rest in place *(above, left)*. Take the nailing strip off a new piece by scoring and snapping it, then use tin snips to cut this piece so it overlaps the existing siding by 3 inches at each end. Apply butyl gutter seal along the remaining part of the old piece and press the new piece in place *(above, right)*, hooking it into the interlocking edge of the siding below it. Hold or prop the piece until the adhesive dries.

When planning to paint a masonry wall or foundation that is cracked or has damaged joints, you'll need to make the necessary repairs to create a sound painting surface and an attractive finish.

In mortared walls, most problems occur at the joints. Mortar can shrink or break down. Eventually it will need to be removed and replaced. Freeze-thaw cycles in cold climates, excess moisture, and settling can add to the problem.

Cracks of up to $1/8$ inch in a concrete foundation are common and usually not cause for concern; hairline cracks as well as slightly wider cracks can be patched as shown on the following pages. However, if a crack is wider than $1/8$ inch, causes leaking, or has edges that aren't parallel, it may be a sign of a structural problem. Have these cracks inspected by a professional.

Repointing damaged mortar joints

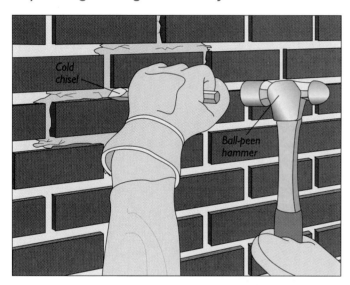

1 Removing the damaged mortar
Wearing safety goggles, chisel out the cracked and crumbling old mortar with a cold chisel and a ball-peen hammer *(left)*, exposing as much of the mortar-bearing faces of the bricks as possible. (Fresh mortar won't adhere well to old.) Expose the joints to a depth of at least $3/4$ inch, then thoroughly brush them out using an old paintbrush.

2 Filling the joints
First, dampen the area. Although you can make your own mortar, it's easier to use dry packaged mortar available at building supply stores. Use weather-resistant type N for exterior walls and follow package directions to mix stiff mortar. While the bricks are still damp, but not shiny wet, use a joint filler or small pointing trowel to fill the joints completely *(right)*. A hawk will help you hold the mortar. Mortar is caustic, so wear work gloves.

3 Tooling the joints

When the mortar is just stiff enough to retain a thumbprint, the joints should be tooled, or "struck." Striking the joints compresses the mortar, waterproofing the joints and contributing to the strength of the wall. Draw a joint striking tool over the joints (*above*). A steel rod or a pointing trowel also can be used.

4 Cleaning up the joints

Cut off any tags (excess mortar) by sliding a trowel along the wall (*above*). Then, restrike the joints as in Step 3. When the mortar is well set, brush the wall with a stiff brush or broom. Keep the joints damp for about 4 days so that the mortar can fully cure.

Patching a crack in concrete

1 Chiseling out the crack

Some concrete patching compounds do not need any surface preparation; others require that you chisel out the crack. Use a cold chisel and a ball-peen hammer or hand-drilling hammer to chip away any damaged concrete (*right*); wear work gloves and safety goggles. Chisel out the crack to about 1/4 inch in width and 1/2 inch in depth; try to undercut the edges (*inset*). If the crack exposes rebar (steel reinforcement), chip out the concrete to 1 inch behind it. Finally, brush out any loose material with a stiff brush.

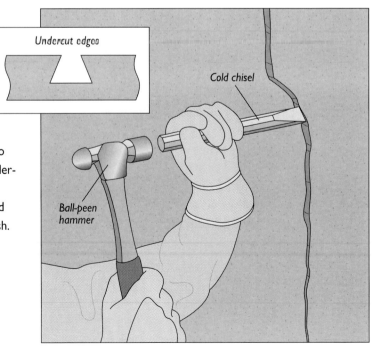

Undercut edges

Cold chisel

Ball-peen hammer

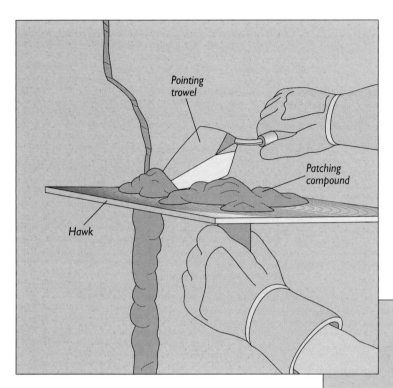

Pointing trowel

Patching compound

Hawk

2 Filling the crack

Fill the crack with latex concrete-patching compound. Some products require a bonding agent that can be applied with a paintbrush—check label instructions. Hold the compound next to the wall on a hawk and fill the crack using a pointing trowel *(left)*. Work from the bottom to the top of the crack, packing in a little more compound than the crack will hold. Make sure to completely fill any space chiseled out behind rebar.

3 Finishing the patch

Scrape off any excess patching compound with the trowel *(right)*. Start at the top and hold the hawk below the trowel to catch the material. Then, smooth the patch with the back of the trowel, starting at the top of the repair. You can use a whisk broom to texture the patch to match the existing wall. Unless you've used a bonding agent, moisten the patch with a mist of water when the edges begin to dry, then cover it with plastic to cure it according to the manufacturer's instructions.

Pointing trowel

Smoothed patch

PATCHING A HAIRLINE CRACK IN CONCRETE

Begin by using a stiff brush to clear out any dirt from the crack. Next, fill the crack with latex concrete-patching compound using a putty knife; apply a little more compound than the crack will hold. Then, go back with the putty knife to scrape off the excess compound. Dampen the patch with a light mist of water when the edges start to look dry. Finally, cover it with plastic and let it cure for the number of days recommended by the manufacturer.

FLASHING

Flashing is sheet metal or roofing installed at locations vulnerable to water seepage. Any leaks that show up around flashing should be repaired before you paint the exterior of your home. You should also try to prevent leaks by checking for breaks in the seals at the edges of the flashing and resealing them.

Renail any loose nails and cover all exposed nailheads with roofing cement. Also plug pinholes with roofing cement; patch holes up to a diameter of ³/₄ inch with the same material as the damaged flashing. First, roughen the area around the hole with a wire brush or sandpaper, then wipe the flashing clean.

Cut a piece of flashing material two inches larger than the hole on all sides. Apply roofing cement to the area; press the patch in place and hold it for several minutes. Cover the patch with another layer of roofing cement. Have a professional roofer replace any flashing that has a larger hole or is badly damaged.

Repairing flashing

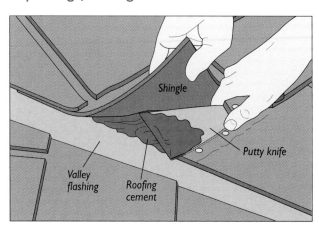

Fixing valley flashing
Lift the edges of shingles along the flashing and use a putty knife to spread roofing cement on the flashing to about 6 inches in from the shingle edges *(left)*.

Restoring chimney flashing
Chip out old mortar and caulk along cap flashing using a cold chisel and a ball-peen hammer. Caulk joints between the chimney and cap flashing, and between cap and step flashings *(right)*.

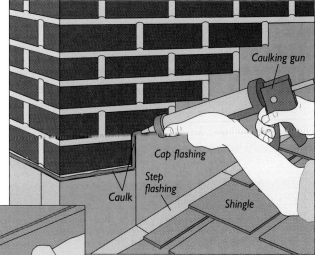

Repairing a self-flashing skylight
Lift adjacent shingles and liberally spread roofing cement between the skylight flange and the roofing felt with a putty knife *(left)*.

Ladders and Scaffolding

Most exterior painting projects will require at least one ladder—if not several different ladders—as well as scaffolding units for different parts of the house.

Aluminum ladders are stronger than their wooden counterparts. They are particularly recommended when you require an extension ladder. There are three grades of aluminum extension ladders, measured by how much weight they can hold: residential, commercial, and industrial. A commercial-grade ladder provides a good balance between strength and light weight.

While it's possible to save money by renting ladders, unless you are very sure of the rented equipment you should think seriously about buying your own. Certain flaws in older ladders may not be visible and when you're standing above the ground you want to be sure that you can trust your ladder.

Fear of heights is a common trait. If you are at all uncomfortable at

Ladder Safety

Ladders and scaffolding should always be used with great care. Keep the following safety tips in mind:

• Position ladders on solid ground (always avoid wet or slippery surfaces), making sure that they don't lean to one side. If the ground is not level, equip the ladder with levelers (see opposite page) and adjust them.

• To steady a ladder—especially when you are working close to a corner of the house—secure it with a rope tied to a tree or other immovable anchor.

• Keep ladders away from power lines; be extra careful with aluminum ones—the material conducts electricity.

• Never stand higher than the third-highest rung of an extension ladder or the second-highest step of a stepladder.

• Keep at least one hand on the ladder as you paint—on an extension ladder, hang the paint can from a rung with a hook; place the paint can on a stepladder's utility shelf.

• Never overreach to one side when you're on a ladder.

• On an extension ladder, make sure the hooks that support the top section are secure and face away from you as you climb.

• If you can't position an extension ladder without leaning the top of it against a gutter, insert a piece of 2-by-4 into the gutter to help prevent it from buckling under your weight.

Positioning a ladder
Placing a ladder too close or too far away from a wall can be dangerous—if it's too close, the ladder may fall backwards; if it's too far away, the ladder may slide out from under you. To determine the correct distance from the wall to set the base of the ladder, place it so that with your arms fully outstretched you can comfortably reach the rung closest to shoulder level, as shown at left. An alternative way to ensure proper ladder positioning is to make sure that the distance from the base of the ladder to the wall is about one-quarter the total length of the ladder.

heights, you're better off hiring a professional to paint the upper reaches of your house.

If you want to do the job yourself, the safest option is to use scaffolding *(below)*. You can order it from a rental agency and have a representative show you how to set it up. Inspect all components carefully, rejecting pieces that are rusted, bent, or have damaged welds.

With two extension ladders (commercial or industrial grade), doubled 2-by-10 wooden planks, and two ladder jacks set at the same level on opposite ladder rungs, you can make a simple, convenient scaffold. However, since these units have no safety rails, they are dangerous and should be used only by people with experience working at heights.

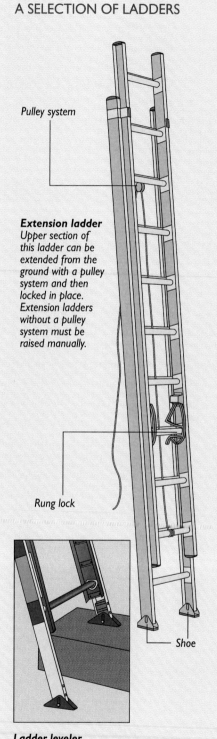

A SELECTION OF LADDERS

Pulley system

Extension ladder
Upper section of this ladder can be extended from the ground with a pulley system and then locked in place. Extension ladders without a pulley system must be raised manually.

Rung lock

Shoe

Ladder leveler
Designed to be adjusted for uneven surfaces, ladder levelers replace standard ladder shoes.

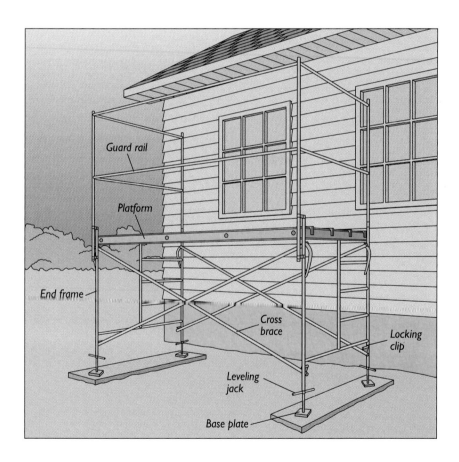

Guard rail

Platform

End frame

Cross brace

Locking clip

Leveling jack

Base plate

ANATOMY OF A SCAFFOLD
Each scaffolding unit consists of end frames, cross braces, frame couplers, locking clips, base plates, leveling jacks (for minor height adjustments), prefabricated decking or wooden planks, and guard rails. The number of units required depends on the height at which you'll be working. To ensure stability on the ground, base plates should rest on 2-by-10 planks. Additional scaffolding levels must be secured to the house. Do this by mounting eye screws in the wall and tying the end frames to them with nylon rope.

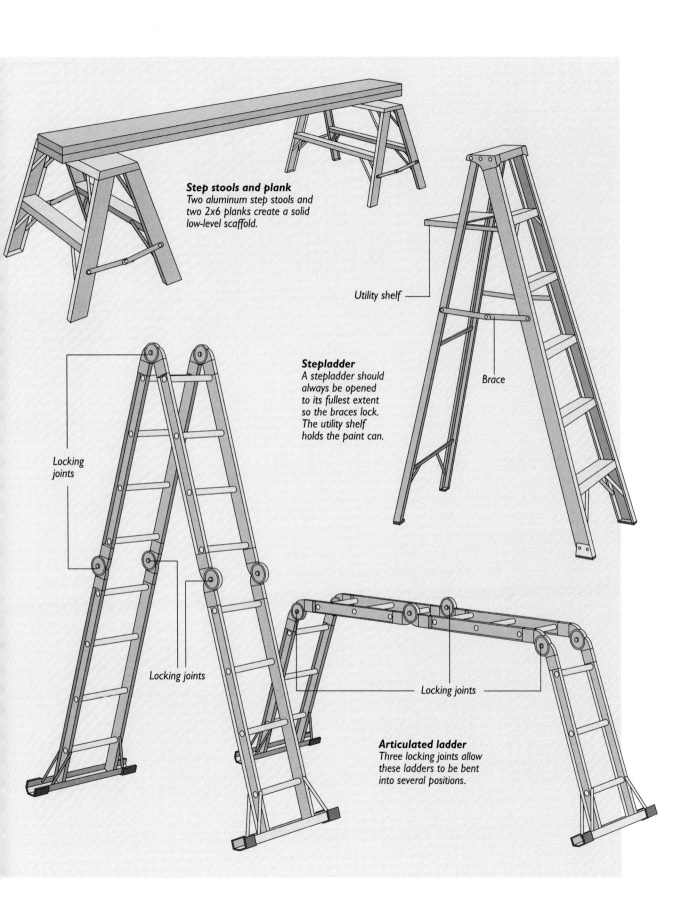

Step stools and plank
Two aluminum step stools and two 2x6 planks create a solid low-level scaffold.

Utility shelf

Stepladder
A stepladder should always be opened to its fullest extent so the braces lock. The utility shelf holds the paint can.

Brace

Locking joints

Locking joints

Locking joints

Articulated ladder
Three locking joints allow these ladders to be bent into several positions.

Painting Techniques

Once you have made all the necessary repairs and prepared the surfaces, it's time to paint.

Even if you have little painting experience, it won't take too long for you to become comfortable with a paintbrush. Still, there is more to exterior painting than simply brushing on paint. The tips and techniques included in this section are intended to get you started on a sure footing and help you avoid the problems that most often frustrate nonprofessional painters.

Your painting project will go more smoothly if you work systematically, concentrating on one section of the surface at a time (an area roughly 3 to 4 feet square when painting a wall, for example). This keeps your attention focused and makes it easier to keep a "wet edge." Maintaining a wet edge is crucial to avoid lap marks—the patchy areas where wet paint or stain was applied over a painted or stained area that was partially dry. When painting horizontal siding, complete two or three boards at a time, work

ing from side to side and keeping a "wet edge." On vertical siding, complete two or three boards at a time from top to bottom. Never stop for a rest in the middle of a surface. Work to a natural break such as a window frame. Whenever possible, work on the shady side of the home to avoid painting in direct sunlight. Painting your home's exterior in the correct order also is critical to creating a good finish. The proper sequence is outlined below.

Before you begin any exterior project, protect the area under where you will be painting with drop cloths. Use tape to mask roofing or other surfaces that will not be coated but may be splattered with paint. Both techniques are shown at right.

Unless you are painting bare wood, carry a scraper with you as you paint in case you come across small areas of loose paint you missed during surface preparation.

Let a wall dry fully before deciding whether touch-ups are required. A paint finish often will look patchy or uneven until it has fully dried.

PAINTING IN THE PROPER ORDER

For the best possible finish, paint the exterior of your home in the following sequence: Begin with gutters, eaves, and fascia boards, then paint the siding. Next paint gutters and downspouts, trim (including around windows and doors), and shutters *(page 187)*. Paint exterior doors and windows using the techniques described for their interior surfaces *(page 54)*. Paint railings next *(page 185)*, then finish the job by coating the porch, if any, and the foundation.

Masking
Cover surfaces adjacent to where you are painting with 3-inch masking tape. When the job is completed, remove the tape.

Fascia

Shutters

Drop cloths
No matter how carefully you work, paint will drip and splatter. Cover plants and shrubs with drop cloths. The best are thick cotton sheets designed for that purpose, although many painters use old bed sheets.

POWER SPRAYERS

Power sprayers can save you time and produce very good results (although this can be messy work—despite what some TV commercials would have you believe). While there is some disagreement among professionals as to whether sprayed surfaces are as durable as brushed surfaces, most agree that if it is applied properly a sprayed finish will last just as long.

The most common paint sprayers are known as airless sprayers and are made in a variety of sizes. These are available at most building supply stores at a reasonable cost; they also can be rented. Because airless sprayers can be difficult to wash, they are best used on larger jobs. Smaller units, or householder spray guns, are suitable for smaller jobs.

In general, sprayers are particularly useful for painting surfaces that are difficult and time-consuming to paint successfully by hand. Ornate molding, wicker furniture, and picket fences are just a few examples. Instructions for effective spraying are given below. Once you have loaded the sprayer with paint and have begun to work, never leave the sprayer idle for more than 20 minutes or the paint will begin to harden, making the parts difficult—or impossible—to clean.

When you have finished painting for the day or are taking an extended break, clean the paint from the unit according to the manufacturer's instructions.

Keep safety in mind as you work. The jet of paint from a sprayer can be powerful enough to force paint through your skin. If you are hit by a stream of paint from close range, get medical attention immediately.

To avoid mishaps or injury when using a power sprayer, always wear eye protection and gloves, and cover yourself up well. Before you clean or repair a power sprayer, turn off and unplug the unit, then pull the spray-gun trigger to release the remaining pressure in the hose. In addition, make sure to set the safety lock on the spray gun when you're not spraying. Keep the spray gun away from children.

Using a power sprayer
Test the sprayer on a large piece of cardboard, adjusting the unit to get a uniform spray pattern with minimum pressure. This saves finish and helps prevent excess paint (and particularly stain) from drifting through the air and covering inappropriate surfaces. To get a smooth even coat, keep the gun about 10 inches from the surface as you spray a succession of overlapping strips. Move the sprayer at a constant speed—about 3 inches per second. Spray straight at the surface as shown at near right; avoid swinging your arm back and forth so the gun moves farther away at the end of each swing. A portable cart-mounted sprayer is shown at far right.

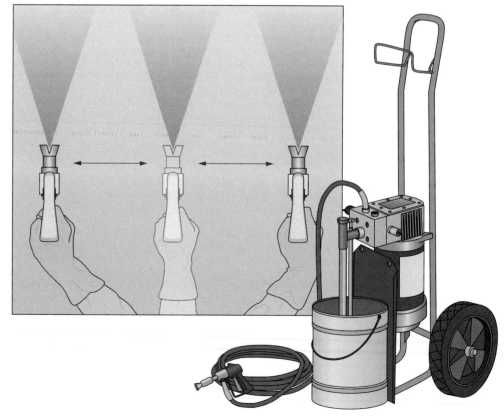

Painting siding

1 Painting the edges

Working in 3- or 4-foot-square sections, begin by painting along the bottom horizontal edges of the siding boards (right), painting against the bristles as explained on page 185. To prevent drips and lap marks, start at a top corner and paint horizontally all the way across 3 or 4 boards. Dip the brush no more than 1 inch into the paint can or bucket since you will not need a fully loaded brush as this stage.

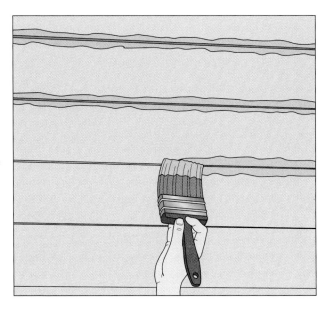

2 Painting the open surface

Dip the brush about 2 inches into the paint to get more paint on the brush. Tap the brush against the side of the bucket to clear paint from one side. To keep most paint on the brush, turn the brush parallel to the ground as you lift it. Quickly press the paint-heavy side of the brush against the surface. Spread the paint in a side-to-side motion over an increasingly larger surface (left) until the paint no longer provides adequate cover at the edges. Where the wood grain of the siding runs vertically, smooth the paint with vertical strokes (see below).

Smoothing out paint on vertical grain

If the grain of the wood you're painting runs up and down, such as on wood shingles, smooth out the paint by brushing with the grain (right). This prevents the brush from leaving noticeable bristle marks in the finish.

Paintbrush Tips

• After painting for a while, the bristles next to the brush's metal band will become thick with paint and start to drip. Clean them by dragging each side of the bristles over the rim of the paint can a few times, or scrape the brush against the edge of a siding board and smooth out the excess paint onto the surface.

• As you paint, check for drips and streaks every 15 minutes or so and smooth them out immediately. Once the paint has dried, these imperfections will be much harder to hide. If you find a drip after the paint has started to dry, wait 24 hours after painting and cut it off with a putty knife, slicing carefully from bottom to top. (The paint will be dry, but the drip will still be soft enough to cut.)

• The larger the brush you use, the faster you'll get the job done. A 4-inch brush is the best choice for wide surfaces but, with some practice, you can use wide brushes for more intricate work—window sashes and narrow moldings—by painting against the bristles *(page 185)*.

• On rough surfaces, don't be afraid to press and squish the brush against the surface, thereby forcing out more paint, to provide a complete cover as quickly as possible.

• If you've just washed a brush and want to reuse it right away, first dry it until damp. Use a brush spinner *(page 56)* or, for a brush washed in water, a hair dryer.

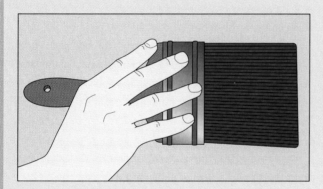

Holding a brush
Instead of wrapping your hand around the paintbrush handle, for certain jobs—like painting siding—you will find the grip shown at left to be more comfortable. Gripping the brush with your whole hand restricts the movement of your wrist. The grip shown here allows you to swivel and angle the brush throughout the brush stroke without moving the rest of your body.

PAD APPLICATORS

Pad applicators offer an alternative to brushes and rollers, and come in various designs for different surfaces.

Applicators with a pad of short, soft, nylon bristles work well on uneven surfaces such as shingles. Use the same basic technique as with a paintbrush. First, apply paint to the edges of the shingles with the edge of the pad. Then, paint the shingle faces by pressing the paint-loaded pad against them and pulling it downward in one stroke.

Applicators also are available with a thick, spongy backing that adjusts to meet rough or undulating surfaces like brick and other masonry units. Work the paint into the surface with a circular motion and smooth it out with straight strokes.

Brushing techniques

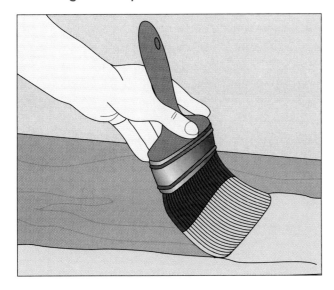

Painting with the bristles
Paint with the bristles of the paintbrush when covering flat surfaces wide enough to accommodate the brush. Pull the brush as shown at left, dragging the bristles with moderate pressure over the surface.

Painting against the bristles
Paint against the bristles in tight or rough spots such as the lower edge of a siding board *(page 183, Step 1)*. As you angle the brush, wiggle and press the bristles to make sure you get enough paint on the surface as shown at right. Painting against the bristles can leave streaks in the paint so you may need to smooth the finish by painting with the bristles.

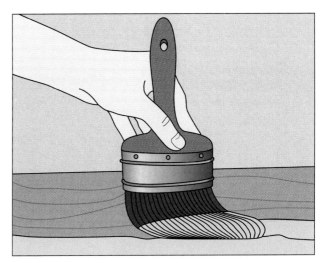

A painter's mitt for railings and pipes

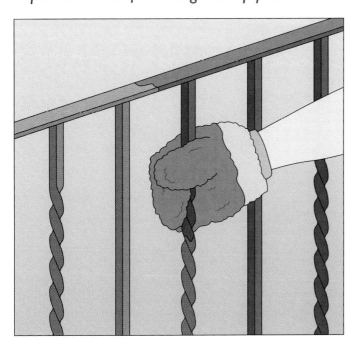

Using a painter's mitt
When you need to paint railings or narrow pipes, a painter's mitt can do the job more quickly than a regular paintbrush. With the thick, soft mitt on your hand, dip it into a paint tray. Then, simply grasp the pipe or railing *(left)* and slide the mitt over the surface; reload the mitt as required. Note: Painting with a mitt can be messy. Before starting, ensure that all nontargeted surfaces are well protected.

TRIM AND SHUTTERS

Trim: Trim is any board that surrounds a window or door, or runs vertically or horizontally along the side or length of a house.

If you plan to paint the trim on your house a different color from the siding, wait until the siding is dry before beginning. Although this will take longer—requiring you to go over the same areas twice—you will avoid mixing together different colors of wet paint and won't have to work with two sets of paint brushes and paint cans.

It is easier to paint trim with the same type of paint used on the siding. While you can switch from latex to alkyd or vice versa when painting trim, by keeping to the same type of paint you won't have to keep track of different drying times or which brush should be washed in water and which should be washed in solvent.

Perhaps the most painstaking part of painting trim is doing the edges next to the siding. You can

Painting trim faces

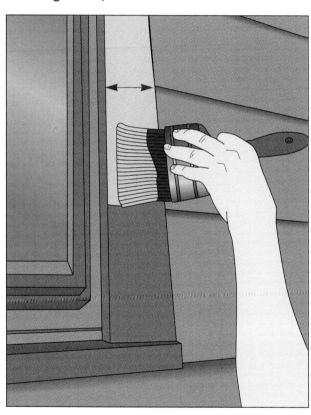

1 Painting perpendicular to the grain
To ensure the trim face is well covered, begin applying the paint by brushing perpendicular to the direction of the wood grain. Start at the inside edge and paint toward the siding *(left)*, lifting the brush off the board just as you reach the other edge.

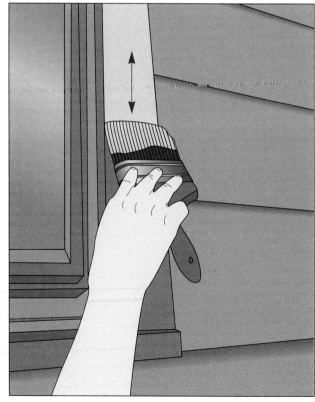

2 Painting with the grain
To smooth out the paint and create an even cover, finish painting the trim by brushing with the grain *(right)*. Turn the brush diagonally to the trim if it is too wide to avoid getting paint on the siding.

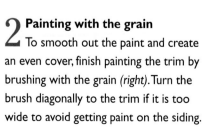

save a lot of trouble by painting this part of the trim the same color as the siding. However, if you feel this will detract from the look of the final finish, use masking tape to protect the siding. Remove the masking tape soon after painting.

Because painting trim is comparatively delicate work, have a supply of cloth rags on hand to wipe up any spills or streaks.

Shutters: Shutters are more easily painted once they have been removed. You will have already done this if they needed to be scraped and sanded.

If you have many louvered shutters to paint, consider using a power sprayer—you will finish the job in a fraction of the time (see page 182).

To spray shutters, prop them against a plank placed atop two sawhorses (drape a drop cloth over the plank and protect the surrounding area with additional cloths). Spray each shutter working from top to bottom, angling the

APPLYING EXTERIOR STAIN

Exterior stain requires no primer and is easier to apply than paint. Stain can be applied to new wood, wood that is sanded clear of paint, and surfaces previously painted with stain. Stain cannot be applied over paint because paint creates a finish that is too dense to allow the stain to sink in. In a short time, the stain will simply fall from the surface.

One disadvantage of stain is that it fades more quickly than paint, requiring more frequent recoating. However, by applying two or more coats at one application, you can extend the life of the finish considerably.

Avoiding lap marks (the shiny or patchy areas where wet stain has been applied over the edge of a section that has already dried) is more difficult with stain than with paint because stain dries more quickly. An added frustration is that you cannot see lap marks until the surface has dried. Once lap marks become visible, the only way to eliminate them is by adding another coat of stain. Keeping a wet edge and adding a second coat of stain are ways to reduce the likelihood of lap marks.

To make it easier to keep a wet edge, stain small sections of the surface at a time. This will make it less likely that the edge of the section you are painting will dry before you can extend it by staining neighboring sections. If you need

to take a break, stop staining at the edge of a siding board or at some other natural break on the surface.

If you apply two coats of stain, the first will seal the surface. This, in turn, allows the second coat to dry more slowly because it will not be absorbed into the surface. (Wait 24 hours to apply the second coat.) This also will help you maintain a wet edge for a longer period.

Because successful staining jobs must be completed quickly and because stain is thinner than paint, staining can be messy. As the stain drips down the surface, catch it with the brush and smooth it onto the surface. A stain brush, which is wider and has shorter bristles than a regular paintbrush, helps control dripping because it holds less finish while increasing the area covered by each stroke.

As you work, be sure to mix the stain at regular intervals as the pigment can begin to settle quite quickly. Working from a 5-gallon bucket will make stirring the stain less messy. Mixing several cans together in a bucket also will eliminate any slight color variations between cans of stain. You can pour stain from the bucket back into a can to transport it more easily.

Clean up stain as you would paint. For alkyd stain, soak brushes and wash out the bucket with thinner; for latex stain, clean with water.

nozzle upward slightly so the paint gets between the louvers. To spray the sides of the frame, adjust the sprayer so you can apply paint from just a few inches away. Paint the top edge of the shutter with a brush and the bottom when the rest of the shutter has dried. Check the shutters 10 minutes after painting them and smooth out any drips with a brush.

When you paint shutters with a brush, begin by painting the joints where the louvers meet the frame, then paint the louvers. Next, move onto the frame. First paint against the grain before smoothing out the finish by painting with the grain.

Check the shutters for drips; smooth them out with the brush.

To carry a wet shutter, insert two screwdrivers under a louver and lift it carefully. Arrange drying shutters like a house of cards, standing them on end and leaning them together so they touch at a single point on their edges.

Cleaning Up

Painting and staining can be messy work. By placing drop cloths or masking tape over all surfaces and objects that could be splattered by paint, you can avoid many potential problems *(page 180)*. Still, you invariably will get paint where you don't want it. In addition to the following tips, refer to the information on cleaning up starting on page 56.

Cleaning clothes: Don't bother trying to get paint out of your work clothes. They probably will be beyond saving and of little use except for future painting projects. However, if someone accidentally brushes against a newly painted surface, you should be able to remove the paint from the affected garment if you act quickly enough.

To wash out latex paint, rub the spot with soap under running warm water. For alkyd paint, rub in a mechanic's hand cleaner from both sides of the garment and rinse under warm water. Repeat, if necessary. In both cases, follow hand-washing by cleaning the clothing in the washing machine. Don't use thinner to wash clothes since this may damage the fabric.

Cleaning roof shingles: Spilling paint on the roof can make quite a mess. The angle of the roof can cause paint to flow for an extended distance. To prevent this from happening, act quickly and throw a rag or drop cloth onto the paint to stop the flow. As the paint pools in front of the cloth, scoop up as much as possible with a paintbrush and put it back in the can. Wipe up the paint with clean rags.

Carefully clean the area of latex paint with water; use thinner for alkyd paint. A stiff-bristled scrubbing brush can be useful. As much as possible, avoid spreading the mess around as you wash. Continue to add thinner or water and continue scrubbing until the spot fades. Since you will likely be left with a discolored patch, let it dry and cover it with a matte spray paint of a color that matches the shingles. If you can't find a compatible spray paint color, you may need to replace the discolored shingles.

Cleaning screens: To remove paint from a screen, dab away as much of the wet paint as possible with a cloth rag or paper towel, making an effort not to spread the paint around. Pour some mechanic's hand cleaner on another rag or towel and push the cleaner through the screen. While holding the rag or towel in place, have a helper wipe off the cleaner from the other side of the screen. Repeat the process from opposite sides of the screen.

Index

Acknowledgments

The editors wish to thank the following:

Diane Capuano, Paint and Decorating Retailers Association, St. Louis, MO

Dameon, ICI Canada Inc., Concord, Ont.

Russ Day, Palomar Builders, San Diego, CA

Maril Hamilton, The Design Consortium, San Diego, CA

Jim McRae, Griffintown Media, Montreal, Que.

William Mills, Montreal, Que.

Marlene Pearce, Marlene Pearce and Associates, Riverview, N.B.

Barbara Richardson, ICI Color Design Studio, Cleveland, OH

Contributing Art Director:

Jean-Pierre Bourgeois

Contributing Illustrator:

Panama Design

The following people also assisted in the preparation of this book:

Lorraine Doré, Angelika Gollnow, Pascale Hueber, Jennifer Meltzer, Valery Pigeon-Dumas, Roberto Schulz

Picture Credits

7	Jean-Claude Hurni
9	(upper) Phillip H. Ennis/Design: Anne Cooper Interiors, Inc.
9	(lower) Crandall & Crandall
10	(upper) Phillip H. Ennis/Design: Saunders & Walsh, Inc.
10	(lower) Phillip H. Ennis/Design: Van Hattum & Simmons, Inc.
11	Philip Harvey
12	Phillip H. Ennis/Design: Eleanor Leonard Associates
15	Kenneth Rice
16	Phillip H. Ennis/Design: Gail Green II Inc.
17	Phillip H. Ennis/Design: D'Image Associates
18	Phillip H. Ennis/Design: George Constant Interiors
19	Jean-Claude Hurni
20	Tom Wyatt
21	Philip Harvey
22	Philip Harvey
23	Phillip H. Ennis/Design: Ronald Bricke & Associates
24	(left) Philip Harvey
24	Phillip H. Ennis/Design: Geneviève Fauré Interior Design
25	Phillip H. Ennis
26	(both) Patrick Barta
29	Philip Harvey
30	Kenneth Rice
31	Kenneth Rice
33	Phillip H. Ennis/Design: Frog Hollow Interiors
34	Phillip H. Ennis/Design: Ronald Bricke & Associates
35	Jean-Claude Hurni
60	Phillip H. Ennis/Design: Anne Cooper Interiors, Inc.
61	Phillip H. Ennis
65	(upper left) Philip Harvey
65	(lower right) Jean-Claude Hurni
66	Phillip H. Ennis
67-82	Tom Wyatt
84	Tom Wyatt
85	Tom Wyatt
88	Phillip H. Ennis
91	Philip Harvey
92	Crandall & Crandall
118	Philip Harvey
124	(both) Jean-Claude Hurni
125	Phillip H. Ennis/Design: William B. Johns & Partners, Ltd.
130	Phillip H. Ennis/Design: Robert Metzger Interiors
132	Phillip H. Ennis/Design: Justin Baxter
133	www.davidduncanlivingston.com
134	Phillip H. Ennis/Design: McMillen, Inc.
136	Philip Harvey
137	Phillip H. Ennis/Design: Saunders & Walsh, Inc.
145	Phillip H. Ennis/Design: Cynthia, Inc.
146	Jean-Claude Hurni
149	Jean-Claude Hurni
150	Jean-Claude Hurni
151	Jean-Claude Hurni
152	(upper left) ICI Canada Inc.
152	(lower left) Kenneth Rice
152	(right) ICI Canada Inc.
153	(all) ICI Canada Inc.
154	(all) ICI Canada Inc.
155	(upper left) Kenneth Rice
155	(lower left) ICI Canada Inc.
155	(upper right) ICI Canada Inc.
155	(lower right) Kenneth Rice
160	Crandall & Crandall
166	Jean-Claude Hurni